FIGHTING FOR LOVE:

TURN CONFLICT INTO INTIMACY

FIGHTING FOR LOVE:

TURN CONFLICT INTO INTIMACY

A COUPLE'S GUIDE

Mari Frank &
Leonard Szymczak

Porpoise Press

Praise for *Fighting for Love*

"Mari Frank and Leonard Szymczak offer a brilliant book for transforming relationships. Mari's expertise as a mediation attorney and Leonard's skill as a psychotherapist help shine the light on forgiveness, healing, and intimacy."

~ Marci Shimoff, #1 *New York Times* bestselling author
of *Happy for No Reason, Love for No Reason,* and
Chicken Soup for the Woman's Soul

"What could be more rewarding than turning conflict into genuine intimacy? In this clear, practical, and life-changing book, Mari Frank and Leonard Szymczak combine their experience as mediator and psychotherapist to show couples how to stop destructive patterns, negotiate win/win solutions, and rediscover love and intimacy. Highly recommended!"

~ William Ury, coauthor of *Getting to Yes* and
author of *Getting to Yes with Yourself*

"Couples that continually fight over who's right or who's to blame are simply digging their own deep chasm of separation. Let Mari and Leonard support you in building an indestructible bridge of love and connection. If you're interested in authentic intimacy, then read this book, or even better, read it together!"

~ Thomas Crum, author of *The Magic of Conflict,*
Journey to Center, and *Three Deep Breaths*

"The secret to relationship success is not how deeply you care for a person, but how compassionately you respond to the bumps in the road: the conflicts, disagreements, and disappointments. This excellent book, written by two seasoned experts, shows you how to turn fragile love into lasting love, and how to turn any fight into a win-win story for everyone."

~ Mark Waldman, executive MBA faculty, Loyola
Marymount University, and coauthor of
Words Can Change Your Brain and *How
Enlightenment Changes Your Brain*

"Countless couples are miserable or break up for two reasons: They gave up on love and increasing conflict drove them apart. *Fighting for Love* is a book that eloquently, effectively, and sometimes humorously solves this. If you long for intimacy but live in conflict, this book is just what you need."

~ Dr. Lee Jampolsky, psychologist and bestselling author
of *Smile for No Good Reason*, www.drleejampolsky.com

"The ultimate expression of love is forgiveness. I have helped many couples create a more intimate relationship, stronger than the one that brought them almost to a divorce, by practicing both forgiveness of the other and forgiveness of self. This book helps couples forgive and is a must read for every relationship with love challenges."

~ Azim N. Khamisa, founder/CEO of the Tariq Khamisa
Foundation and author of *From Murder to Forgiveness*,
www.azimkhamisa.com

"Mari and Leonard offer many useful tools to navigate the complexity of transforming conflict into an ongoing, loving relationship. They show it is possible to recognize and heal our early wounds and to give and receive the love we truly desire."

~ Joan Gattuso, bestselling author of
A Course in Love, A Course in Life,
The Lotus Still Blooms, and *The Power of Forgiveness*

"As you read *Fighting for Love*, you will easily feel the passion and love that went into writing this book. It's a thorough, easy to understand book on how to navigate through, and even benefit from, the inevitable relationship conflicts we all go through. The exercises throughout the book will help you apply the wise and clearly written words. I highly recommend this book!"

~ Todd Creager, author of *The Long Hot Marriage*

"*Fighting for Love* is, above all, a useful book, as the authors combine the twin insights and methodologies of mediation and psychology. They reveal practical bridges that can easily be crossed by couples seeking to transform their conflicts into insights, intimacy, and improved relationships. They list hundreds of ways couples can end destructive patterns and constructively turn their conflicts into positive directions."

~ Kenneth Cloke, author of *The Crossroads of Conflict*
and *The Dance of Opposites*

"*Fighting for Love* is a roadmap to understanding what it truly means to connect with another on an intimate level of love and harmony. Unmet expectations set the stage for bitterness and conflict in relationships. The authors have presented a "love guide" to teach how acceptance of self opens the door to a future of long-lasting love. Let this book be your guide to the deep intimacy you so desire."

~ Barbara Miller, bestselling author of
You Lost Your Marriage Not Your Life

"For anyone wanting to improve their relationship with their partner, Mari Frank and Leonard Szymczak's book is a real find. Every chapter is rich with relevant tips on how to restore a loving connection. I highly recommend *Fighting for Love*. It should be on every couple's nightstand."

~ Nancie Kohlenberger, coauthor of
The Couple's Guide to Thriving with ADHD

"I've often had the thought that the world would be a much better place if people automatically saw conflict happily — as but the springboard to clarity, authentic self-expression, and genuine connection. Mari and Leonard have created a fresh, humane, and hopeful guidebook to make this a reality. Wow!"

~ Nancy Dreyfus, PsyD, author of *Talk to Me Like I'm Someone You Love: Relationship Repair in a Flash*

"What a gem of a book! *Fighting for Love* shows you how to implement positive lasting change in your intimate relationship. Mari and Leonard openly share their personal relationship stories, demonstrating the power of positive change and healing. If you want to fight for love, do it right and buy this easy-to-read, excellent book with common sense tips. You'll love it!"

~ Dr. Margot E. Brown, author of *Kickstart Your Relationship Now! Move On or Move Out*

"Mari and Leonard's new book helps you determine who you are, as an individual and as a partner in your love relationship. If you're all right with that — and if not — you can still fight for love."

~ Robert DesJardins, Esq., family law specialist and author of *Passing Through*

"*Fighting for Love* is wise and well-written. The coauthors, a mediator and a therapist, reveal complementary perspectives. When emotions get triggered, it's easy to repeat harmful patterns from childhood but much better to nurture the relationship and communicate constructively about challenges. Many examples show how to do this. The cartoons throughout the book add a light touch to a serious subject. They made me laugh out loud."

~ Marcia Naomi Berger, MSW, LCSW, author of *Marriage Meetings for Lasting Love: 30 Minutes a Week to the Relationship You've Always Wanted*

"Read this book! It offers life-changing strategies to rebuild your relationship. Mari and Leonard share their wisdom, stories, and loving attitude to help you replace drama with forgiveness, trust, and compassion—the recipe for extraordinary heart-filled relationships."

~ Danna Beal, author of
The Extraordinary Workplace: Replacing Fear with Trust and Compassion

Other Books by Mari Frank

From Victim to Victor

Safeguard Your Identity

The Complete Idiot's Guide to Recovering from Identity Theft

Negotiation Breakthroughs (privately published)

Other Books by Leonard Szymczak

The Roadmap Home: Your GPS to Inner Peace

Cuckoo Forevermore

Kookaburra's Last Laugh

Disclaimer: This publication is meant to provide information about relationships. It is not meant to replace therapy, mediation, or legal advice. Each couple has unique concerns and should seek professional advice when appropriate.

Library of Congress Cataloging-in-Publication Data
Frank, Mari and Szymczak, Leonard
Fighting for Love: Turn Conflict into Intimacy — A Couple's Guide
Published by Porpoise Press, Laguna Niguel, CA

LCCN: 2016947517

ISBN-10: 1-892126-88-5
ISBN-13: 978-1-892126-88-7

Cover Design: Fiona Jayde
Interior Design: Tamara Cribley
Author photograph for Mari & Leonard: Lifetouch Portraits
Cartoons: Randy Glasbergen
Editor: Mary Harris

Published by Porpoise Press
Laguna Niguel, CA

1. FAMILY & RELATIONSHIPS/conflict resolution.
2. PSYCHOLOGY / Psychotherapy / Couples & Family.
3. FAMILY & RELATIONSHIPS / Love & Romance.
4. LAW/Family Law/Marriage.

DEDICATION

Mari

To my parents, Sondra and Philip Bear, who
knew how to fight for love and stay together for
almost fifty years until Sondra's passing.

To my children, Alyssa and Bryan, who
laugh even when they quarrel.

To my loving husband, Lloyd D. Boshaw, Jr.,
who has graciously committed to grow and
enhance our love by fighting for love with me
as we become more mindful of who we are and
what we want in our marriage.

Leonard

To Ingrid Starrs, who acted as a mirror to help me
see all that I am and can be. I am grateful for her love,
compassion, and generosity.

To my children, Melissa and Nate, who bless me with
their kind hearts and loving spirits.

Table of Contents

FOREWORD

Couples fight. We know this. But many escalate their fights into a separation and divorce. And that's it.

Others barely fight at all and drift apart. Now that no-fault divorce has been the law of the land for over forty years, splitting up is relatively easy to do and often feels like the best way to go. Friends, family members, and even professionals often encourage separation and divorce as a way to stop fighting.

While divorce rates have been dropping slightly to less than half of marriages, fewer people are getting married and unmarried couples split up even more easily. We're living in a time of relationship reluctance, yet almost everyone says they would prefer to be married and happily so, if they only had the right partner.

Into this context comes a new and refreshing look at couples fighting by Mari Frank and Leonard Szymczak. Rather than simply saying that fighting is a normal part of any couple relationships, they go many steps beyond. Instead of treating a fight as a bad sign, they say to use that energy as a gift. "Embrace conflict as a growth opportunity." Use the "spark of energy" that conflict triggers to help you grow more intimate and passionate.

In this book they give you the skills to accomplish this task. And skills are the key, I believe. The "right" partner is one who's willing to learn and grow with you. If partners learn the skills in this book, they have a much better chance to become the right partners themselves.

But Frank and Szymczak don't just give lots of tips to help learn these skills; they also give many sample conversations, insights, thought questions at the end of each chapter, and tons of encouraging words.

What a wonderful book for couples, whether just starting out or dealing with conflicts that already seem overwhelming. *Fighting for Love* gives couples a sense of hope, a larger perspective on managing conflicts and passionate ways to learn about and support each other. This book shows you how this can really work!

William A. ("Bill") Eddy has been a family lawyer for over 23 years, after being a family therapist for 12 years. He is president of the High Conflict Institute based in San Diego. He is the author of several books including *It's All Your Fault! 12 Tips for Managing People Who Blame Others for Everything* and *It's All Your Fault at Work! Managing Narcissists and Other High-Conflict People* www.HighConflictInstitute.com

There is no way to peace; peace is the way.

– A. J. Muste

"Of course I can accept you for who you are.
You are someone I need to change."

INTRODUCTION

So what is discord at one level of your being is harmony at another level.

–Alan Watts

The only thing worth fighting for is love. But when we fight with our loved one, we feel isolated and disconnected. So, why did we name this book *Fighting for Love*?

Ironically, we experienced disagreement with others over the title of this book. We first wanted to call it, *The Gift of Conflict*, because, in essence, we learned that conflict can be a gift that transforms us from separation into connection. However, when we shared the proposed title with friends and colleagues, they were confused. Many didn't like the title. Who would want to open a gift with conflict inside? We reconsidered and recognized that lovers need to fight for the love that they want so they can be more passionate and intimate.

We even had a disagreement between us over the cover art of this book. Mari wanted a red rose between red boxing gloves in the shape of a heart on a white background to signify passion. Leonard wanted a white daisy between a red and blue boxing glove to signify, "He /she loves me; he/she loves me not." We collaborated and came up with a better solution. You will notice that we have a yellow daisy between red and blue boxing gloves on a white background. We are both pleased and still friends. The conflict created a better result.

What does it mean to fight for love? It means that we commit to do whatever it takes for love, even if it means ending a relationship. That means wrestling with our own thoughts and emotions that keep us from loving ourselves and getting the love we desire with our romantic partner. In writing this book, we thought about the meaning of love in our own lives and this forced us to look within and change ourselves. It made us conscious of how we treat our partners and how we wanted to be treated. Each of us became more conscious of how we fight to love and accept ourselves and our partners. Here's part of our journey.

Mari's Fight for Love

I grew up in a suburb of Chicago in the gangster-infiltrated town of Oak Park, Illinois. My parents were children of the Depression, and each single-handedly supported their large families to survive. After they married, they continued their workaholic habits, laboring long hours together in their fur store for almost forty years until they retired. They worked, ate, and slept side by side, twenty-four hours a day. As Aesop would say, "Familiarity breeds contempt."

Having to fend for myself as a little girl, with my parents unavailable and an absent busy, older sister, I felt abandoned. When my parents would return home from a difficult day, I would use my intuitive mediation skills to divert their bickering in a cute little girl way. I was trying to get the attention and love that I needed as a latchkey kid. Although they quarreled during much of their time working together, when they finally retired, they became more loving and accepting and took care of and supported each other. They were married for almost fifty years until my mom died.

The abandonment that I felt as a child became a pattern, which would eventually play out in my first marriage. When I married a partner who was not comfortable communicating his emotions, I felt abandoned again. Our inability to connect led us to quarrel and become distant.

While teaching high school and simultaneously working other jobs, I supported my husband for the first eight and a half years of our marriage while he obtained his medical degree. After I earned my Master's Degree, my husband started his residency and we finally had our son. I had hoped that we could re-devote ourselves to each other and our family to connect at a deeper level. However, we further disconnected.

I turned my attention outward to fulfill my need to bond with others. I immersed myself in the community by getting elected to a school board and teaching at the university level, as well as going to law school. This caused more discord because I still felt abandoned by my husband, and, at that point, he felt abandoned by me. We didn't have the skills to reconcile our feelings and turn the conflict into intimacy.

After I became a lawyer, we decided to have our daughter, believing that our growing family would save our marriage. But although my legal skills developed, our relationship deteriorated.

Our marriage ended after eighteen years. Although I felt devastated and again felt abandoned and alone with two small children, my dark night of the soul awakened me. I realized that I had to explore my contribution to the breakdown of our marriage. I stopped blaming my ex-spouse and sought counseling to get insight, change myself, forgive him, and be free of the negativity of the past. I learned to be more conscious of my thoughts and my part of the disconnection. I wanted to be a positive role model for my kids, to have a romantic partner in my life again, and to help my clients move more positively through the challenges of a marital dissolution.

I recognized that the blame and guilt mentality that was prevalent in my marriage ruined our relationship. Sadly, the foundation of our entire judicial system, based on blame and guilt, tears all relationships apart. With that epiphany, I immersed myself in mediation training to enable people in conflict to arrive at a fair and peaceful legal settlement. Acquiring the skills of facilitating collaborative dispute resolution helped me to heal and set me on my quest to assist others in the midst of agonizing conflict.

While recovering from my divorce, I met my current husband, Lloyd, who was suffering from his own divorce. We both had felt like "dumpees," abandoned and betrayed by our spouses. Together, we spent hours reading aloud relationship books about how to help us build lasting love. We now have been married fifteen years, but together for twenty-seven years. Although we still face conflict *opportunities*, we continue to work through issues, share challenging emotions, and journey through life's joys and tragedies. We understand that our conflicts, although never comfortable, enable us to fight for enduring love.

Conflict in any relationship is an opportunity to grow. Getting to know and work with Leonard has forced me to honor diverse approaches. With his wisdom and humor, he challenged me and my views. Although we didn't always agree, we used the tools in this book to respectively hear each other and resolve our differences. Thank God, our tools worked!

Leonard's Fight for Love

My four grandparents who emigrated from Poland experienced the conflict of discrimination and a language barrier as they settled in Chicago. Both of my parents lost their fathers before they were five. That created a life of struggle that continued after they married.

My father left the family when my mother was pregnant with me. He returned but the battles continued. After they separated, they continued their fierce arguments. My two sisters, brother, and I were caught in the middle of two warring camps. I had hoped that my parents could relate to each other in a peaceful manner. That never happened. My turbulent childhood laid the groundwork for my interest in conflict and instilled within me the quest to create peace and love in relationships.

I experienced love off and on in a marriage that lasted twenty-six years. During part of that time, my wife and I lived in Australia where our two children were born.

Conflict arose about divergent needs. I wanted to remain in Australia, whereas she was called to move back to Chicago and be with her family.

In Australia, I was a director of a marriage and family center and worked with couples and families who were trying to find their way through the maze of conflict that arose from different cultures and ethnic backgrounds. It became quite evident that no matter the background, the source of all problems in relationships begins with our own thoughts. They can be healed by changing our perceptions and our thinking.

This became more evident when my family returned to Chicago. I went through a difficult divorce, which forced me to examine my beliefs and change the way I thought. I recognized that I still carried embattled fragments from childhood. When fearful, I would resort to self-protection. My fear of abandonment and neglect played out in my unconscious programming.

After the divorce, I recognized that conflict offered a gift to see parts of myself through my partner. I had experienced early in life that relationships were about struggle. When life became easy and effortless, I unconsciously self-sabotaged to create struggle to reinforce my self-fulfilling prophecy.

I now see that conflict acts as a trigger to remind me to become aware of my thoughts and perceptions. If there is tension, I have the choice to either stew in the emotions or seize the opportunity to learn about myself. Every relationship I have had revealed aspects of myself. Some I liked and some I didn't. However, each reflection helped me to evolve and grow.

After my divorce, I spent nineteen years on my own and had several relationships. I was commitment-phobic, fearing the loss of my freedom. Yet, each relationship helped me face the barriers that prevented me from lasting love. I did independence and self-sufficiency well, so I had to learn to be more interdependent and express my desires more clearly. That's when I met Ingrid Starrs. She joined me on the journey of fighting for love. She helped me open my heart and see how I show up in love. I saw my ongoing struggle with managing my conflicting needs for togetherness and separateness. I felt like a rubber band, stretching out to connect toward intimacy. When I over-adapted and over-accommodated, familiar feelings I had as a child, I would snap back toward independence. After regaining my sense of self, I would try and reconnect. I recognized that rubber banding in relationships was very common for men. As this book goes to print, I am still working out this rubber banding process with Ingrid. No matter what happens, I feel indebted to her for helping me evolve and turn conflict into intimacy.

This book collaboration with my dear friend, Mari, has reinforced the power of fighting for love. We came together to share insights about relationships and present workshops. Mari's passion and dedication to bring peace into the world continues to inspire me. I am excited that we can share these powerful techniques with you.

Mari and Leonard

In our collaboration, we found that we approached disputes from two perspectives. In her mediation practice, Mari works with clients from the outside in, facilitating positive ways for them to speak and act with one another, which then alter their internal attitudes and feelings. Leonard deals with clients from the inside out, helping them understand their inner feelings, which changes their thoughts and emotions, resulting in new actions and behaviors. Our practices exemplified the Yin and Yang of couple's conflict resolution. Instead of viewing our approaches as opposite, we have come to see them as powerful and complementary to bridge the inner and the outer worlds.

We created this book so you can fearlessly and confidently know that you can deal with any conflict in your relationships. We will show you how to use it to enhance your love life. We hope you will resist any tendency to blame, accuse, withdraw, avoid, impose guilt, or control your loved one. If you commit to fighting for love in a mindful way, you will battle against anything that blocks you and your partner from getting the love you deserve. We look forward to guiding you on the journey to transform conflict into greater intimacy.

Every conflict we face in life is rich with positive and negative potential. It can be a source of inspiration, enlightenment, learning, transformation, and growth—or rage, fear, shame, entrapment, and resistance. The choice is not up to our opponents, but to us, and our willingness to face and work through them.

– Kenneth Cloke and Joan Goldsmith

"Why are you so afraid to commit? Do you really think you're going to meet someone better than me?"

OVERVIEW

Love does not resolve every conflict; it accepts conflict as the arena in which the work of love is to be done.

— Daniel Day Williams

Marla and Jack lived together for seven years. They professed their love for each other, but lately, it seemed they bickered all the time. They blamed each other for a lack of romance, not spending quality time with each other, and for starting fights. They both craved a love connection, but both felt frustrated. They didn't have the tools to fight for love.

Have you ever felt like Marla and Jack, where conflict diminished your love connection? Their conflict was a call to fight for love and evolve as individuals and as a couple. Are you willing to fight for long-lasting love? If the answer is yes, this book will give you simple strategies, steps, and exercises to build a better relationship.

No matter how much you love your partner, eventually your unique experiences and viewpoints will become apparent, and you will have disagreements. Different perspectives, styles, needs, and even goals can cause conflict. Feeling disrespected, unloved, offended, or degraded can cause conflict to escalate.

If we react to our loved one by criticizing, blaming, inducing guilt, or acting in ways that cause hurt and anger, we end up in a battle over who is right, instead of fighting for the love we crave. Fighting for love means that we put energy into resisting anything that gets in the way of creating a loving, respectful connection. To fight for love means that we will not let anything unlike love get in the way of our intimate relationship.

The poet Rumi wrote, "Your task is not to seek for love, but merely to seek and find all the barriers within yourself that you have built against it." This requires us to recognize our defenses and fight the tendency to blame. It takes courage to admit our part in any conflict. To deeply connect, we need to learn to accept each other with our imperfections and vulnerabilities and discover a bond between our authentic selves. To do that, we must understand and accept ourselves first. Then we take responsibility for our part of any relationship challenge.

We believe that our very essence is love. When we peel back the layers of negative and fearful emotions and become mindful of our thoughts and actions, we awaken to who we really are and what we want. Knowing and loving ourselves enables us to treat our loved ones with respect and dignity, even if they may not agree with what we say or what we want to do. Genuine love doesn't proclaim, "If you do what I want, that shows me that you love me, and then, in return, I will love you back." Mature lovers respect each other's different needs, desires, and opinions, and give each other the gift of understanding.

Where did we learn how to be intimate partners? Most of us haven't had successful role models of loving relationships. We were not taught in school how to behave in an intimate partnership, except from sex education classes, which only dealt with what happens during the physical act of making love. In addition, most of us didn't learn conflict resolution skills at home, at school, or in the workplace. It's no surprise that in America one out of two marriages end up in divorce.

If we want to create long-lasting loving relationships, we must acquire effective skills. In this book, we will give you concrete tools to help you bond emotionally, intimately, and deeply with your partner. The techniques and skills will help you on your journey to turn conflict into intimacy. In the process, you will come to believe, as we do, that conflict is a gift in disguise.

How can conflict be a gift? When difficulties arise in our relationships, they cause us to question what is going on. They call for introspection, self-discovery, and force us to grow. Quarrels can serve as vehicles to foster greater understanding and new insights about ourselves and how we relate. The gift in conflict comes with the resolution and our evolution.

How we react to conflict creates either a positive or negative outcome, depending on how we deal with it. Tension may cause us to transform and change, or it can cause us to retreat, get stuck, or become hostile. Conflict is a call for change, but if we engage in battle, or if we fear or resist it, conflict escalates into chaos. When we collaborate with our partner and address the underlying causes, we can reach satisfying solutions.

Imagine your life without issues to resolve, difficulties to manage, or even differences between people.

On first blush, it may sound like nirvana. But, how would you evolve, mature, and discover your talents, skills, and inner strength? If everyone always agreed with you, and you were never challenged, you would stagnate.

We have written this book to help you and your partner positively transform your relationship. We have created twelve chapters that take you through a process that will deepen your awareness of how you presently deal with clashes with your partner. We will show you more effective alternative approaches to deal with your struggles so you will actually get closer. We include exercises at the end of each chapter to give you a chance to apply and practice the concepts in your own relationship.

Chapter 1. "What's the Gift in Conflict" shows you how every fight with your loved one holds an opportunity to enhance your connection and evolve together.

Chapter 2. "Why Do You Fight?" examines how your childhood affects your current relationship, and what you can do to move past the challenges to create the love you have always wanted.

Chapter 3. "What Do You Need and What Do You Want?" explores your own needs and desires and offers effective ways to communicate and mutually satisfy each other.

Chapter 4. "Who Am I? Who Are You?" provides insight into your own personality style and that of your partner, and how best to communicate to reduce conflict.

Chapter 5. "Stop the Destructive Patterns" identifies your own patterns of avoiding or engaging in arguments, so you can replace them with successful approaches to handling differences.

Chapter 6. "Boundaries: Stay On Your Side and I'll Stay On Mine" shows you how to establish appropriate and respectful limits to insure security, protection, and safety in your relationship.

Chapter 7. "Build Bridges: The Love Connection" walks you through ways to build bridges of connection between you and your loved one and establish a closer bond.

Chapter 8. "Forgive Me Not; Forgive Me" teaches you a process to release past hurts, overcome resentments, and renew your love connection.

Chapter 9. "Change Your Thinking, Change Your Love Life" helps you recognize how you can change your thought and beliefs to improve and enhance your love life.

Chapter 10. "What's the Solution? Make Me a Deal" offers a simple, yet effective step-by-step approach to work through relational challenges and reach an agreement.

Chapter 11. "Transform Hostility with Hard Love" presents powerful strategies to overcome pent-up hostility and resentment so you can reignite your loving feelings.

Chapter 12. "Heal from the Inside Out" shows you how to heal from relationship pain, whether or not you and your partner are still together.

Engaging in the exercises at the end of each chapter will give you a chance to apply the tools and techniques in the book. We encourage you to try them with your partner. However, if that is not possible, do them by yourself. Be lighthearted as you complete them. Avoid criticizing or judging yourself or your loved one. The goal is to help you discover new insights that bring you and your partner closer.

There always will be conflict in our relationships because each of us is a unique human being. As Thomas Crum wrote in *The Magic of Conflict*, "Conflict can be seen as a gift of energy, in which neither side loses and a new dance is created." So embrace conflict as a growth opportunity to create a deeper level of connection and a more satisfying way of being in a relationship.

In the middle of difficulty lies opportunity.

– Albert Einstein

CHAPTER 1

What's the Gift in Conflict?

Every problem has a gift for you in its hands.

— Richard Bach

S ally and Michael fell in love at first sight and soon moved in together. Two years later, they began to criticize each other. One evening when Michael arrived home late for dinner, Sally approached him angrily.

> Sally: *You're always late, and you don't even bother to call. You've ruined our dinner. The chicken is now overcooked.*

> Michael: *You're nagging again. If dinner is ruined, it's your own fault.*

What could be the potential gift in this uncomfortable situation? At this point, neither partner got what they needed from each other. Both felt alienated and hungry. Dinner was ruined and they surely didn't want to go out for a meal together!

If Sally and Michael understood their own feelings and their behavior, they could describe their concerns in a more tolerable manner. Increased understanding and a renewed connection would be possible if they took responsibility for their emotions and consciously spoke to each other without imposing guilt. Fighting for love isn't about bickering with each other. Rather, it is about fighting against the internal knee-jerk reaction to negative emotions. The challenge for Sally and Michael is to recognize what the fight is all about — the battle *inside* their minds and the communication clash *outside* with their partner.

We see this dispute from two perspectives: the yin and the yang of conflict. The yin and yang are Chinese principles that describe two opposing forces. The yin is the receptive force, while the yang is more active. In actuality, they are complementary and interconnected. Both are necessary and give rise to the other. We're using yin to represent the inside thoughts and feelings and yang to symbolize the outward communication and behavior that creates interactions.

Let's first look at the situation from Sally's point of view from the yin perspective or inside out. She felt angry about being disrespected because Michael didn't value her time or efforts. Her feelings of hurt, abandonment, and being unloved rose to the surface because he was late, yet again. She even worried that he could have been with another woman. That provoked fear and insecurity.

Michael's situation from the inside out was equally upsetting. He felt angry, blamed, and unjustly accused, when in fact he worked late and got stuck in traffic. He arrived home tired and hungry, and faced a rubber chicken for dinner.

All these inner feelings made it difficult for the couple to manage their ill feelings and remain in control of their responses. If they had paused and taken a breath, they could have turned inward and asked themselves these questions:

- What am I feeling?

- Why am I reacting so strongly?

- What do I really want?

From an inner place of calm, they could have thought through their response so that their lover could hear them. Neither partner wanted to be criticized, condemned, or rejected by the other, and they certainly didn't want a war. However, when they allowed their emotions to rule, their interactions became out of control.

What they really wanted was understanding, appreciation, and mutual respect. Sally also wanted cuddling and Michael wanted sex! None of that happened!

Now let's look at their behaviors from the yang, the *outside in*. Sally's tone of voice, pointing finger, and blaming words elicited an accusative response from Michael. He yelled, leaned forward, and criticized Sally for being a nag. Their behaviors alienated each other from the love they craved.

There were many ways that Michael and Sally could have handled this situation. They could have used one of the strategies or skills outlined in this book to produce a positive outcome. One simple step to deflect conflict would have them refrain from using the word "you" when expressing a negative statement. Saying the word "you" in conjunction with a concern is often perceived by the listener as guilt inducing. Blame and criticism evoke anger and resentment. However, using "you" with a compliment does just the opposite, it fosters affection. When bringing up a challenging situation, using "I" Messages opens the door to peacefully resolving disagreements.

If Sally and Michael assumed responsibility for their inside emotions and mindfully had chosen non-offensive words and behavior with each other, they would have fostered understanding and perhaps even humor about the fate of the chicken. The scenario below is one replay of how the parties could have used "I" and positive "You" Messages to address the conflict.

Sally: *Michael, I'm glad you're home. I feel upset when I don't get a call letting me know what's happening. I became totally distracted and overcooked our dinner. I would be grateful if you would call me in the future to let me know you are okay.*

Michael: *I'm sorry for being late. I had a deadline to meet. I'll call you next time. You're a sweetheart for understanding. I guess I better take you out to dinner, or else we'll be forced to eat that rubber chicken.*

Was there a gift in this conflict? When this couple reviewed what had happened, they recognized their inner feelings and chose to speak without blame or criticism. They showed mutual respect and were able to reconnect. Sally received an apology, and Michael made a commitment to tell her when he would be late. The couple hugged and went out for a romantic dinner.

If you cringe when you think of your own disputes, consider these questions:

- How could you change your own blaming statements to get a positive response from your partner?

- How could you be more mindful when your partner criticizes you?

- What if you could accept that conflict in your love relationship is a catalyst for you to use positive words to connect?

- What could be the gift for you and your partner in your next disagreement?

When you view conflict as a transformative tool, it becomes a gift. You can release the fear of arguments and create communication that fosters a greater understanding of each other. The key to fighting for love is to become aware of how your mind works, how your emotions influence you, and how old patterns of thought and your previous actions contribute to your present challenges.

What is Conflict?

The word "conflict" comes from the Latin word *conflictus*, meaning "a contest." A contest denotes a challenge that brings about change. There is one constant in this world. Everything changes — the weather, seasons, cars, and bodies. Nothing stagnates. Accepting change, adapting, and being open and receptive to embracing it allows us to be in the flow of life. Conflict initiates change.

Consider the many magnificent changes caused by conflict in nature. The caterpillar's body experiences conflict when it breaks down the cells to bring about a metamorphosis as a beautiful butterfly emerges. A snake labors in conflict as it fights to release its old skin to reveal a shiny new one. The clashing forces of a forest fire make way for rich soil and a healthy new grove. Scenic beaches are formed by the conflict of shells, boulders, and rocks pounded into crystallized sand. The tension of landmasses pushing up through the earth form majestic mountain peaks. Babies struggle through the birth canal to breathe life. In nature, conflict creates change and growth. Without conflict, there is no transformation.

If we are willing to calmly endure the change that conflict brings, we will receive the gift of growth in ourselves and in our relations with others. As we release our belief that conflict is bad and perceive it as an opportunity for creativity, it will transform our experiences.

Conflict need not be about proving who is right or wrong. It provides insight into acknowledging and appreciating our differences. It enables us to blend ideas and discover new ways of behaving, so we can join together more genuinely. Understanding differences force us to shift our thinking and create within and with others new energy patterns. It generates a relationship wake-up call.

Imagine that you and your partner are having a romantic day, laughing and snuggling, and suddenly, your sweetheart says something that pushes your buttons. Your mind reacts. The negative emotions stir up bad feelings and the positive energy sours. That becomes a critical juncture where the conversation can become hostile, or it can cause you both to stop and become conscious of the shift in energy. You can become mindful together, explore what happened, and clarify misunderstandings. You both can apologize for hurt feelings and connect with a passionate kiss.

The Chinese word for conflict or crisis is comprised of two different symbols: 危機 Wei-chi, "danger" and "opportunity." When conflict brings us to crises, we stand at a crossroad between danger and opportunity. The word conflict has a bad reputation because it is usually associated with frustration, hostility, violence, and war. It also can be hazardous in loving relationships when ignored, avoided, or suppressed. When it induces fear or escalates to rage, it may cause harm and destroy a loving bond. Unresolved relationship conflict is dangerous since it builds intense resentment.

Relationships and marriages often fail because partners haven't learned the skills to seize the opportunity to use conflict as a gift of growth. If couples don't have the tools to build bridges of connection, they end up fighting to win right rather than fighting for love.

Leonard works with couples to break the power struggle that keeps them locked into blaming each other. He helps them to stop trying to change one another. Instead, he teaches them to alter the negative patterns in the relationship. Once the couples "get" that the goal isn't to find fault, but to appreciate each other's differences, they can develop solutions together and build a happier and more satisfying relationship.

Henry and Phyllis had been living together for eight years. Phyllis was twelve years older than Henry and complained that she earned more money in her business. Henry worked as a teacher and his salary didn't compare to his partner's. Even though they had more than enough money, their arguments continued to center around finances and their inability to save. Clearly, they were unable to listen to or understand the other person's perspective. Their battles eventually brought them into therapy.

Initially, each tried to convince Leonard that the other person was causing the problems. Like most couples who enter therapy, each person hoped to change the other, believing that such a change would stop any conflict and lead to happily ever after.

In couples therapy, the goal is to identify relationship problems, clarify each person's expectation and desires for the partnership, and help each person communicate in a healthy way that satisfies their own and their partner's needs. Most individuals want to be heard and understood, and feel cared for and loved. In therapy, they learn to take responsibility for their thoughts and actions.

With Henry and Phyllis, their communication styles created conflict, as both would quickly fall into a pattern of defending their positions and attacking their partner's behavior. Clearly, neither felt heard, understood, cared for, or loved. Therapy helped them recognize what wasn't working and what they could each do to reverse the negative spiraling pattern into a positive uplifting pattern. Since both Henry and Phyllis were committed to staying together, they were prepared to explore with one another how they contributed to the conflict and learn new ways to relate.

After a number of sessions, Phyllis and Henry began implementing the communication strategies outlined in this book. Their interactions became positive, and they were able to create a plan to deal with the money issues. In the process, they both felt more understood and loved.

Unfortunately, some couples are unable to reverse the negative cycle in their relationship and move toward dissolution. Some of those couples end up in mediation to dissolve the marriage. By the time they come to Mari, they have usually experienced years of criticism and hurt, making it almost impossible for the relationship to be salvaged. However, sometimes there is still hope to rekindle love when they are willing to use new tools to communicate and forgive each other.

Sandy and Rick came to mediation after twenty-nine years of marriage and three grown children. They told Mari how they came to decide upon divorce: Rick was a top executive in the insurance industry and Sandy was an emergency room physician. They had been a handsome power couple, entertaining and living an active social life until Rick suffered a heart attack. During his recovery, Sandy was attentive and made sure he was expertly treated by her colleagues. However, Rick became emotionally distraught about his frailty and fear of not being virile enough for his wife. He became distant, uncommunicative, and lashed out at Sandy whenever she approached him. Feeling verbally abused, hurt, and lonely, she begged him to go to counseling. He refused. Meanwhile at work, one of her fellow physicians, in the throes of divorce, asked Sandy to have coffee so they could commiserate about their painful marriages. Soon thereafter, their connection turned intimate. Guilt-ridden, Sandy confessed to Rick. He quickly demanded a divorce.

They decided to mediate their divorce to avoid the nastiness of litigation. They wanted to have a peaceful settlement, but there was enormous resentment. In order to move forward and to collaborate to get an agreement, Mari knew they would have to express deep feelings and forgive each other so that the underlying anger would not interfere with negotiating a positive and fair settlement.

The beauty of mediation, like counseling, is that it is a private process without court reporters or judges. It is a safe place to reveal confidences. Mari asked each of them to tell how they were feeling (using "I" Messages) about Rick's illness and what it meant to each of them. Then she asked them to write down and repeat back to their spouse what they heard. Mari's next step was to ask each of them to apologize for the hurt that the other felt. This helped them let go of the anger. Even if it could not be a total forgiveness at that time, the energy shifted in the room and the tension subsided. They stopped the blame game and were shown how to take responsibility for their feelings and thoughts. This opened the door to exploring the intense emotions around the heart attack.

As the meeting continued, the couple's attitude brightened. They practiced communication skills and engaged in "solutioneering" (described in Chapter 10). They were given tasks to perform and information to gather before the next meeting.

During the next session, Sandy and Rick smiled, and even laughed, as they collaborated effortlessly. After two more meetings, they informed Mari that with their new toolbox of techniques to communicate, they decided to dismiss the petition for divorce. Instead of dissolving the marriage, they decided to fight for love. They rekindled their love through a deep understanding of each other's feelings. They made a commitment to eradicate blame, judgment, and criticism. Twelve years have passed, and they are still together. They experienced the gift in conflict and the healing power of forgiveness.

When you experience conflict with your loved one, the potential gift for you is an awakening. Just as Sandy and Rick gained new insights from their conflict, you can accept conflict as a catalyst for positive change. Consider letting go of your fear of vulnerability and become conscious of your emotions and actions. You may ask yourself, "What am I thinking and doing that contributes to this problem?" The answers can reveal new insights on how you can change your approach and communicate more effectively and compassionately.

Are you ready to fight for love?

Conflict creates a spark of energy that has the potential to transform into intimacy and reignite passion. Successfully resolving arguments strengthens the bond between you and your partner. Exposing the hidden parts of yourself through a safe dispute resolution process helps both of you grow and heal as a team.

The Beatles song "All You Need Is Love" may be inspiring, but couples who don't know how to positively address disagreements soon learn that love is *not* enough. Falling in love is fueled by sexual attraction, affection, and emotional connection. As time passes, love can only be maintained by trust, respect, compassion, intimacy, understanding, and forgiveness. If couples allow conflict to escalate dangerously as prolonged anger, hurt, and resentment, the ensuing heartbreak and sadness may demolish the relationship.

When we are immersed in the infatuation stage, we don't anticipate heartaches or breakups. During that falling in love phase, conflict is usually avoided while the chemical factories in our brain produce intense attraction and bonding chemicals. As we join as a couple, we literally get high on love. Testosterone, serotonin, dopamine, oxytocin, and pheromones help us feel "in love." Infatuation keeps us together to explore common values, desires, and interests, and of course physical intimacy.

Once we have bonded, the infatuation phase shifts to another stage that is often represented by a struggle with power and control. We take off the blinders and realize that our partner does not always share the same tastes. We may recognize different philosophies, styles, goals, or aspirations. This offers us opportunities to work through issues, clarify communication, and establish roles and a relational vision. If we can move through the storm, we establish greater cohesiveness and deeper intimacy. If we can accept each other's differences, we develop a higher degree of loyalty, support, and joint decision-making. We even come to appreciate our individual talents and differences.

This book intends to move you through power and control issues toward a deeper level of intimacy so you experience real love, which is about feeling free to be yourself. When differences in perceptions become evident, you can rekindle that passionate love, and reboot the chemical factory in the brain, so you can each be supportive of your uniqueness yet still be mindful of one another's boundaries.

Unlike a beautifully wrapped present, the gift disguised in conflict is not encased in elegant packaging. Instead, it is often deeply hidden within messy challenges. As we consciously peel off the unattractive layers of negative emotions and the old patterns that no longer serve us, we will relate more authentically. We will learn to skillfully fight off the offensive reactions that block us from bonding more deeply. Then our gift of connection emerges.

If you still aren't convinced that conflict is a gift, recall a time in your life when you experienced challenges and difficulties that were emotionally trying, yet you overcame those problems triumphantly. Whether you endured a painful recovery after an accident, bounced back after a business failure, endured the death of a loved one, survived a life-threatening disease, or moved beyond a painful divorce, you found the strength to rise above life's arduous experiences and achieve victories. Overcoming and processing painful situations can be life altering in amazing ways.

During dark times, you may have wanted to retreat and hide. You probably experienced anger, denial, and grief, but you found courage and thrived. You discovered that you were stronger than you thought you could ever be. You learned about yourself when you overcame great obstacles. The saying "the greater the pain, the greater the growth" often rings true. Painful journeys present gifts that create renewal.

Exploring feelings of the past, recognizing your emotions, and engaging in new ways of thinking offer transformational gifts. With insight, courage, wisdom, and a renewed appreciation for your partner, your fight for love will set you on a quest to become more aware of who you are as a human being and as a partner.

In the next chapter, we will explore the origin of your inner conflict. But first, we invite you to participate in an exercise.

FIGHTING FOR LOVE EXERCISES:

After each chapter, we present exercises to help you reflect on your life. Questions raise awareness and insight, which precede change. Questions can also promote a dialogue with your partner. You can complete the exercises on your own, or if your partner is open to sharing ideas with you, review the answers together. This opens a conversation for new insights.

If you are practicing this with your lover, organize a time to share your answers without judgment. Bring a sense of curiosity. Afterward, thank each other for sharing. The revelations help you whenever you experience a relationship challenge.

1. Describe your feelings when conflict arises with your partner.

2. What is your lover's emotional reaction to conflict?

3. How does your partner's reaction make you feel and act?

4. How do you feel about the way you presently deal with conflict?

5. Describe what you would like to see you and your partner do in the future when you have a disagreement.

"We were made for each other. I needed new
luggage and he came with a lot of baggage."

CHAPTER 2

Why Do You Fight?

*What may appear as Truth to one person will often
appear as untruth to another person ... Where
there is honest effort, it will be realized that what
appeared to be different truths are like the countless
and apparently different leaves of the same tree.*

— Gandhi

After ten years of marriage and constant arguing,
Roberta and Fred sought counseling. Roberta
decided to move into the spare bedroom until
she and Fred resolved their problems. Needless to say,
their sexual relationship froze. Both blamed the other
and felt hopelessly trapped in a relationship that continually drained them. Their marriage headed toward
divorce.

Couples like Roberta and Fred feel frustrated and
powerless when they become caught in the web of conflict. They often believe that their partner is the cause of

their pain and anguish and wish that the other would change. "If Fred acted differently, I would be happy."

Although we may fight about money, relatives, chores, time together, or sex, many of our fights are really about disconnection. The first step to unravel the tangled web is to understand the complex nature of conflict.

When we experience internal conflict about our underlying needs, desires, feelings, and decisions, we carry that conflict into our relationships. If we are ambivalent about what we need or want, how can we expect our partner to understand us? That's why it is so important to recognize our needs and wants so we can be clear with our partner. We will deal with this more fully in Chapter 3, What Do You Need and What Do You Want?

Most of us in relationships focus on the clashes with our partner. The nature of interpersonal conflict is that both parties are trying to get something that they do not have, or they want a different outcome. Conflict is a natural phenomenon. The existence of conflict is not the problem. Instead, it is how we perceive it or negatively react to it that causes problems.

To help us understand more about why we fight, let's look at the evolution of how we as humans resolve conflicts. A tiny baby, attached to an umbilical cord, floats in a warm, nurturing womb. Everything the infant desires — nourishment, protection, and love — are provided. The regulated environment monitors temperature and physical needs. However, when the child leaves the comfort of his mother and takes the first wailing breath, conflict is born. Entering a world of sounds, sensations, and light, the infant must survive by depending not only on the caregivers, but also on the ability to express needs and adapt to an ever-changing environment.

At birth, we arrived with a pre-installed genetic structure and immediately started recording what we saw, heard, felt, tasted, and touched. In the process, we learned about cause and effect. When we acted a certain way, something happened. If we wanted food, sleep, or warmth, we sent a physical signal, possibly through tears or agitation, to communicate our distress. We also learned to expresses comfort and pleasure with smiles and laughter.

We established an attachment to our parents or caregivers that became a building block for trust, safety, love, and security in future relationships. Our very survival became dependent on that bond. If we felt protected and lovingly connected with our caregivers, we learned to be confident that our needs would be met.

Those early memories were carried forward into our relationships. If we felt anxious or fearful as a result of an unavailable, inconsistent, or neglectful parent, we brought those feelings into our present love life.

Over time, we recorded experiences and memories that reminded us when we felt loved or unloved, appreciated or punished. We adopted a language, culture, customs, nationality, and values. Once we began school, we downloaded mental programs about achievement, success, and failure. We learned to accommodate and adapt to avoid pain and receive love and acceptance. From our early life experiences, we developed beliefs about nutrition, sex, pleasure, emotions, self-care, money, roles, and spirituality.

To satisfy our needs for love, acceptance, recognition, appreciation, or safety, we adopted behaviors, emotions, and thoughts. We either accommodated, adapted, withdrew, or rebelled. Through trial and error, rewards and punishments, we learned to survive in the world and satisfy our needs. Behaviors that served needs in the past were continued into the present by sheer habit.

Through our repeated interactions and negotiations with parents and other family members, we developed a relational model. Every time we received love or experienced pain, we stored those memories in a mental filing system. That provided the basis for our world of relationships. We learned to make decisions about cooperating and competing, about conflict and intimacy, and about creating boundaries or dissolving them.

As a result, our powerful, relational programming, which is mostly unconscious, operates in the background in all our interactions. It drives us to select partners and recreate patterns from the past. Whenever we interact with our lover, we encounter that person on many dimensions. In every discussion, we experience our partner emotionally through our senses — how he or she sounds, looks, feels, smells, and even tastes. We unwittingly associate those sensations with memories from the past. If a partner speaks to us in a loud voice, we may be reminded of a parent who yelled at us. Instinctively, we will respond as we did as a child, whether it be placating, withdrawing, or fighting back. If our partner smiles at us in a certain way, we may remember a time when we felt understood and loved.

Some of our internalized memories, when triggered, lead to heartfelt love and intimacy, while others can create distressful feelings of separation. Anguish from the past may lead to power struggles, isolation, co-dependence, or escalated conflict.

Take a moment and think of a time when you felt loved and cherished as a child. How does that image make you feel? Notice your physical responses and thoughts. You may picture your mother or father holding you or speaking to you in a nurturing way. You may experience warmth around your heart and feel appreciated, or grateful that they loved you.

Now imagine an occasion when a parent was angry at you. How do you feel when recalling that angry situation? Notice your physical sensations. You may feel tightness in your shoulders and chest, or have twinges in your belly of guilt, shame, disappointment, or resentment.

Incidents that have occurred in the past still affect us. Stored memories will automatically trigger a response in the present, until we raise our level of awareness. Over time, we will have developed our story about relationships that drives our internal conversation when we are interacting with our loved one. How we perceive our history becomes the framework that shapes the way we view the past, live the present, and anticipate the future. Our internal self-talk, what we think and say in our mind about ourselves and our partners, creates our experiences.

What we tell ourselves establishes and reinforces our story. We become what we think about. If we believe our needs won't be met in a relationship, that we are not good enough or are unlovable, then we will anticipate that our partner will reenact that belief. We then act out our part, which leads to exactly what we fear. This leads to self-sabotage. If, however, we believe that we are worthy of love and that our needs will be met, we will behave in such a way that will create that for us in a relationship. Each of us is the main character in our life story. We can play a victim or an empowered hero, depending on our thoughts, and actions. Each time we tell ourselves a prior belief, we lay a brick to reinforce our internal story. We can build an ugly shack based on old, negative messages from the past that have replayed hundreds of thousands of times, or we can consciously construct a beautiful home with a strong foundation of new positive thoughts that support our desires.

Leonard worked with a client we will call Laura. She struggled in most relationships. She was the eldest of five raised by a single mother who worked in a factory to provide for the family. Since she had to care for the younger children, Laura's life became one of survival and caregiving. When she left home, she unconsciously sought men who needed looking after. After falling into the role of caregiver in one relationship after another, she became depressed, believing she could never have the love she craved, and that she was a loser. The story that she told herself was about being destined to survive with a loveless life. Her self-talk reinforced those beliefs and became a self-fulfilling prophecy.

During the course of counseling, Laura began to recognize that she often felt like a victim. When she let go of the hurt and pain and chose to think differently about herself, she became empowered. From that place of power, she made decisions to be more loving toward herself and to seek a partner who would cherish her.

Instead of telling herself that she was unworthy and unlovable, she nurtured the belief that she was, indeed, worthy of love and that life could be easy. Over time, her new beliefs took hold. She eventually became involved with a man who adored her. Together, they created a loving marriage. Both became conscious of their past conditioning and committed themselves to forging a story where their needs were met.

Like Laura, we all have to wrestle with the past. Inner and outer conflict will emerge when we face triggers that elicit old memories. If we had experienced abuse, abandonment, or neglect while growing up, we would be susceptible to behaviors that trigger those painful memories. When our old emotional injuries or fearful feelings get reactivated, we often respond negatively to our partner. However, with insight we can view the conflict as a gift to raise a past injury into consciousness, so that old wounds can be healed and relationships can flourish.

When Jonathan was a child, his mother would often tell him, "You could've done better." Even if he brought home a good report card, she would say, "You must improve." She herself didn't receive much encouragement as a child and passed on her "not good enough" belief to her son. As a result, Jonathan came to believe the message that he wasn't good enough. His unmet need, like many others who had critical parents, was to feel appreciated. When his partner gave him a message that he should improve, that triggered a "not good enough" feeling and an angry reaction. Jonathan saw his partner as acting just like his mother. He believed he had to stand up for himself, something he rarely did as a boy. Jonathan's conflict reminded him to heal those toxic messages from the past and to realize that he was good enough. From a place of self-acceptance, he could hear his partner without the knee-jerk reaction.

Mari has worked with couples in divorce mediation who have spent years re-enacting their childhood hurts and coping mechanisms with their partners. Very often, one of the partners has a great need to control the other. Perhaps the controller felt abandoned or insecure and found that exerting control over a loved one made him or her feel safe, empowered, and self-confident. That type of relationship may work for a while if the controlled partner has a need to feel protected or taken care of after experiencing a childhood where he or she felt insecure or overprotected by a parent.

Elaine and Rodger were such a couple. Rodger made all the financial decisions and controlled what was spent. He told Elaine what to wear, when she could take a shower, and what food she could buy. Whenever she wanted to exercise her own judgment, Rodger criticized her and berated her. Finally, twenty-five years later after her kids were grown, she felt totally victimized. She could no longer live in that situation. She recalled how she had a similar relationship with her father who had been a police officer. She had rebelled as a child. Now she finally felt she could fight back and get a divorce. During counseling, she learned that her childhood story was about being told what to do. She realized that she had been re-creating those thoughts. She finally had the courage to engage in the dissolution process and feel empowered. As a result of Elaine's request for divorce, Rodger recognized that he was acting like his father who was over-controlling. Unfortunately, this awareness came too late to save his marriage. But it did lead to his decision to change so that he could have a healthier relationship in the future.

When we are drawn together in a partnership, we bring what we have lived as children along with our longing for a loving attachment. Unconsciously, we choose a partner who brings up old issues so we have a chance to heal old wounds and satisfy unmet needs. Unless we become mindful of what we are recreating in our present relationships, we will repeat old patterns. Those patterns will continue until we take steps to alter them.

Sometimes our upbringing creates an expectation of what a relationship should be like. When it doesn't live up to that standard, the ensuing conflict will lead to feelings of alienation from our partner.

In Mari's initial divorce mediation meeting with Sean and Susan, she asked each of them why they wanted to divorce. Sean answered that he realized that Susan never really loved him because she never doted on him, nor did she put much effort into cooking and cleaning the same way as his mother had. Susan was shocked to hear this, since he had never accused her of not loving him before. Sure, she endured his endless complaining that she was not a great homemaker, but she didn't know he thought that meant she didn't love him. Ironically, she then expressed that she felt that Sean didn't love her since he always criticized her and rarely wanted to have "together" play time with her. In her upbringing, her mother worked full-time and didn't have time to do much cooking. On Saturday mornings, she and her four siblings would quickly clean and do chores. Then the family would go to the park or somewhere else to play together. Her idea of a loving romantic relationship was doing things together, like chores, and then having fun, such as hiking, dancing, talking, or making love. It became clear that instead of sharing their inner feelings about what love meant to them, they criticized and blamed each other for the love they desperately wanted and could not get. In their eyes, divorce was the only option.

Most of us are oblivious to the unconscious programming running in the background that affects our choice of a partner. We may find someone who represents what we are familiar with, or if we had a negative experience with a parent, we may choose someone with opposite traits. The power of the programming from our families plays a potent role in our beliefs and interactions. It directs our thoughts, feelings, and behaviors about love, intimacy, control, emotional expression, values, morals, roles, money, sexuality, spirituality, and religion. If only we could delete the old files in our brain's computer that interfere with our present interactions.

Not surprisingly, conflict emerges in our love relationships as we come together with different past histories, personalities, experiences, and families in an attempt to blend into a unit. Our relationship must accommodate individual wants and needs. In the process, we develop a vision, consciously or unconsciously, about how we should relate.

When interviewing couples for therapy, Leonard asks these questions:

- Out of the billions of people on this planet, how did you choose each other?

- What qualities did you really like about your partner?

- Name the time in your relationship when you felt deeply loved.

- Describe your vision for the relationship.

- What childhood pain do you remember?

- What positive emotions from your childhood do you want to nurture in your relationship?

Our relationships are quite complex. We usually begin with a euphoric, loving foundation. We become intrigued with our partner, fascinated with the commonalities and differences. We feel elated about a mutual attraction. Our sex drive forges an intense passion so we can attach to a lover. Those positive feelings bond us together as we learn to communicate our needs, desires, and dreams for the future.

When conflict arises in our relationship, it is a disheartening letdown. Old themes may play out in the background, such as neglect or abandonment from childhood, or rejection from previous relationships. We can react negatively as we have in the past and decide it is our partner's fault. Alternately, we can decide to use the conflict as an opportunity to learn about ourselves and choose to think, feel, and behave differently. Recreating old patterns that don't serve us keep us stuck and unfulfilled. However, through introspection, insight, and positive action, we can recognize our negative emotions and share our awareness with our partner. As we become conscious of what is going on in our internal thoughts, we can genuinely express our desires differently and satisfy our needs.

Remember at the beginning of the chapter, we met Roberta and Fred who were contemplating divorce and sought counseling instead. They argued all the time and their sex life became nonexistent.

In a couple counseling session, Roberta said she experienced Fred as not paying attention to her, just like her parents. She felt neglected and blamed him for not being a good listener. Enraged, she yelled at her husband, "You never pay attention to me!"

Fred said that he felt criticized, like he did as a child, and lashed out, "You're always starting arguments."

Leonard pointed out that Roberta and Fred could keep reenacting their internal stories, or they could stop the hostile escalation. If they committed to halting the arguments, they could learn from the conflict by refraining from blaming and genuinely listening to one another. In a safe environment in counseling, they analyzed how their current situation was reminiscent of their childhoods.

Leonard encouraged the couple to take turns listening and reflecting back what each heard. They were instructed to use "I" Messages when describing their feelings (e.g., I feel criticized when I am yelled at. I prefer to hear what you have to say in a calm voice.). When both had the experience of being empathically heard and accepted, they felt a profound shift. In a magical moment, Fred let down his defenses, looked into Roberta's eyes, and softly spoke to her about his feelings. Roberta gently reached out and touched his hand as he told her what was happening for him.

Fred said, "I got triggered by the same horrible feelings I had as a kid."

Roberta responded in a loving tone. "That makes sense. I guess the same thing happened for me."

The couple then discussed what they wanted for their relationship and how they could bring more love and passion into their lives. Roberta felt closer to Fred than she had in years and decided to move back into the bedroom. Fred felt understood and respected. With their renewed connection, they both felt a renewed desire for physical and emotional intimacy.

Every couple must balance closeness with separateness. There is that fine line to navigate in our relationships between intimate connection and the need for autonomy.

Some couples require extensive time together and find it hard to tolerate differences, whether they are opinions, habits, or rhythms. Other couples need more space and separateness to satisfy their individual needs and enjoy differences of opinions. If one person wants to spend a great deal of time together and the other needs more alone time, they have to negotiate a solution. Too much time apart can create misunderstandings and disconnection, whereas too much togetherness can lead to enmeshment and loss of identity. The stability of the union depends on respecting each person's needs and beliefs and the type of relationship a couple wishes to create.

With cellphones, laptops, and tablets, couples can easily get distracted by technology, leading to misunderstanding. Consider Angela and Anthony, who live together. Their texting is a source of ongoing battles that prevents them from satisfying their need for togetherness and separateness.

Anthony: *I'm going out for dinner after work with the guys.*

Angela: *Fine, sure. Go ahead. Have fun without me.*

When Anthony received the text, he became angry, thinking Angela was having a dig at him. He texted her back.

Anthony: *I will!*

When he arrived home, he told Angela that he didn't like how she "sounded" in her text. He believed she was upset about him wanting to go out with friends. Angela felt a little left out. She wanted to spend the evening with Anthony; however, she knew he needed time out with the guys. She just wanted him to know that she missed him.

Texting presents challenges to communication. After Anthony received the text response from Angela, he could have texted, "Are you sure you're comfortable with me going?" Alternately, a call could have given the lovers a chance to clarify their responses.

If one of us in a relationship needs more separateness, instead of articulating this need, we may unwittingly create conflict to impose distance and freedom. This coping mechanism may help regain a sense of self. When we are aware of the need to have alone time, we don't need to create conflict. The key is to identify and communicate individual needs, wants, and desires.

Conflict serves to recalibrate our relationships through the many transitions that we endure in our lives. For example, studies of naval families showed that conflict arose for some couples before a sailor left for a tour of duty. Disputes or arguments enabled the couple to emotionally separate and avoid feeling the pain of loss. However, when some of those sailors returned, they quickly established an intimate and close bond.

Conflict can also generate heat and passion to force a couple to fight for love. In those situations, conflict serves as a vehicle to reconnect. Some of the naval couples in the study handled an upcoming overseas tour quite differently. Before those sailors departed, they used the remaining moments together to create a closer, intimate bond, with loving memories, in case a tragedy happened while away. However, soon after some of those sailors returned home, they began to argue, using conflict as a way to re-connect and fight for love.

To find the right balance between the need for separate time and togetherness in a loving relationship takes collaboration and communication. Disconnecting through conflict may create an opportunity for some couples to uncover their inner feelings and desires. As they sort through a problem on their own, they can then come together to express them in a manner that promotes a safe climate of intimacy and growth.

Couples in healthy, loving relationships never eliminate all conflict. Rather, they recognize that conflict is a signal that it is time to communicate. To prevent the discord from escalating into a destructive encounter, they manage their emotions, identify needs, and resolve disagreements. They focus on listening to each other lovingly without judgment. This creates a safe environment to speak openly and listen to one another.

Mirroring happens automatically when two people fall in love. They mirror one another's postures and feelings. They start to talk in shorthand and experience those incredible moments of psychic oneness. Daniel Siegel talks about mirror neurons in his book *Mindsight*. "We are hardwired from birth to detect sequences and make maps in our brains of the internal state — the intentional stance — of other people."[1]

In other words, we imitate and resonate not only with our partner's feelings but also with the internal mental flow of a partner's mind. When we have connected so intensely with another, we find ourselves

---

1   Siegel, Daniel J., *Mindsight: The New Science of Personal Transformation*, New York: Bantam, 2010; pp. 60–61.

thinking and saying the same thing at the same time. That's when we feel we have found our *soul mate.*

In addition to mirror neurons firing, a passionate love relationship generates feel-good bonding chemicals. Dr. Daniel G. Amen's book, *The Brain in Love*, highlights attraction chemicals such as testosterone, estrogen, and pheromones; infatuation chemicals like serotonin, dopamine, and epinephrine; and commitment chemicals like oxytocin and vasopressin.[2]

Any disruption in our relationships creates a chemical change in our brain. We feel distress when we argue and, as a result, experience a withdrawal of feel-good chemicals. When we feel disconnected, it is easy to understand how we may tend to see our partner as the cause of our unhappiness.

Let's return to Roberta and Fred. When feeling neglected, Roberta's brain chemicals reacted and negatively affected her physically as well as mentally. A deficit in the attachment chemicals created a feeling of loss and discomfort, resulting in Roberta blaming her husband.

When Fred felt blamed, the detachment chemicals kicked in for him and he retaliated. Sadly, these lovers produced chemicals and neural pathways that promoted detachment. When they reconnect more lovingly toward each other, using positive words and affection, a flood of attracting chemicals reestablishes a positive bond.

Though there are countless opportunities for disagreements to escalate into intense conflict in

2   Amen, Daniel G., M.D., *The Brain in Love: 12 Lessons to Enhance Your Love Life*, New York: Three Rivers Press, 2007.

relationships, the converse is also true. Gently confronting problems with a compassionate heart offers us the chance to bring into the light the old emotional wounds that block a greater connection. If we look introspectively, a crisis gives us the gift of awakening the need to communicate and heal our past hurts. It also gives us a chance to reveal underlying needs so we can ask for what we want. As we better understand ourselves and open up to a deeper understanding of our loved one, we see new ways to communicate and satisfy each other. We then feel greater acceptance, trust, love, and security. Cultivating loving feelings and thoughts transform conflict and change old habits and beliefs. Positive emotions reinforce neural pathways in the brain that further intimacy and produce feel-good chemicals in the body.

In summary, understanding interpersonal conflict can be condensed into nine principles:

1. Interpersonal conflict is a natural phenomenon that can be resolved peacefully. Both parties wish to satisfy their needs, get something that they do not have, or seek a different outcome.

2. As soon as we are born, we adapt to our environment by adopting ways to think, feel, and behave that help us survive.

3. We bring our childhood programming and stories, both positive and negative, into our relationships.

4. We choose, often unconsciously, a partner who represents positive and negative qualities of our parental figures, and look to them for love and healing.

5. We are triggered emotionally by the positive and negative behaviors that remind us of our early childhood relationships.

6. When we enter a love relationship, we establish patterns and a way of relating that is based on old beliefs and behaviors that we bring to the partnership.

7. When we feel threatened and fearful, or our needs are unmet, conflict alerts us that change is necessary.

8. Unless we consciously alter our perceptions, thoughts, and behaviors, and reframe them in a positive manner, we will respond to conflict in a similar fashion as we did as children.

9. As we become aware of our patterns, we can choose to think, feel, and act in a more loving manner.

Take a few moments to complete the Fighting for Love Exercise. The questions will prepare you for the next chapter about clarifying needs and desires. As you learn to satisfy them, you will increase the love and joy in your relationship.

FIGHTING FOR LOVE EXERCISES:

1. If you could summarize your childhood relationship with your parents into a brief story, what would you write?

2. If you could summarize your partner's parent/child relationship into a brief story, what would you write?

3. Name the similarities and differences in each story.

4. How has each story shaped the love in your relationship?

5. How has each story created opportunities for healing and growth?

GLASBERGEN

"I need you, darling. You complete me."

CHAPTER 3

What Do You Need and What Do You Want?

You will be your best self when you take time to understand what you really need, feel, and want.

— Deborah Day

Alice and Rob planned to go out for "Date Night" on Friday evening. Alice was running late. She had to complete an important business report for tomorrow's staff meeting. It took longer than expected, so she called Rob to tell him she'd drive to the restaurant from the office and meet him there. Meanwhile, Rob had arrived home early to get the children settled with the babysitter. When he received Alice's phone call, he got mad about the delay, but didn't mention it. He and his wife had been working hard the past month and needed a night out, away from the children, so they could spend quality time with one another.

When Rob arrived at their favorite Italian restaurant, Alice wasn't there. He sent her a text: *I'm here. Where are you?*

She responded via text: *Sorry. Almost done. Be there soon.*

Judging from Alice's past behavior, Rob knew soon meant thirty minutes. He began to seethe. His stomach grumbled from hunger pains. He ordered a drink at the bar and waited.

Alice finished the report, but knew it needed another hour for the finishing touches. Feeling guilty about being late for dinner, she planned to return to the office after the meal. On the way to the restaurant, she hit every red light and arrived much later than expected. She found Rob nursing his third drink.

Angry about waiting, Rob began drinking on an empty stomach. Alice felt guilty about being late, anxious about completing the important document, and upset that her husband seemed tipsy.

With a scowl on her face, Alice said, "You've been drinking too much."

Rob countered, "Hey, you're late. I'm starving. What am I supposed to do?"

The couple faced a pivotal point. They could stage a raging argument and blame one another, or they could recognize their unmet needs and effectively fight for love.

Alice and Rob both felt the tension. Rob needed food, as well as attention and an intimate night with his wife. He wanted to feel loved and appreciated for arranging the babysitter and the Date Night. He also needed to express his frustration about Alice arriving late, and, in the process, feel understood.

On the other hand, Alice wanted patience and empathy from Rob about the tremendous pressure she felt to complete a critical report for the upcoming meeting. She needed his support and encouragement, as well as his appreciation for the money she earned, so the family could live at a higher standard. She also needed time to express her feelings and be heard and understood.

In addition to their individual needs, the relationship needed stability and security so the family could survive. The couple desired alone time to strengthen their relational bond. They also needed positive communication, for each one to feel valued as they worked through the misunderstandings.

Most conflict occurs in relationships because needs are unmet. Abraham Maslow listed a hierarchy of needs in the form of a pyramid. Our physiological needs form the base. Once we satisfy the basic needs for food, water, shelter, sleep, and sex, we move up the pyramid to fulfill our need for safety and security that we won't be betrayed and can rely on our loved one. When each level of need is met, we reach higher up the ladder of human potential. As we feel safer, we climb toward love and belonging, which entails connection and commitment. From there, we move toward self-esteem and appreciating who we are. The next level takes us to a deeper understanding of the world and how we relate to the world. Finally, we rise to the top of self-actualization where we recognize and acknowledge our thoughts and emotions, accept them, and then choose to release those thoughts that don't serve our highest potential. This leads to self-fulfillment and healthier relationships.

Physical needs are easier to identify, whereas emotional and psychological needs can be more difficult to recognize. We need to feel safe and secure, connected with others, heard and understood, appreciated, loved and cared for. Additionally, we want to express ourselves and communicate and feel competent, adequate, trusted, and trusting. We need communication, mental stimulation, and a purpose in life. On the flip side, we want to be rid of anxiety and fear, shame, and guilt. As we release feelings of rejection, abandonment, and inadequacy, we can love and accept ourselves more and attract unconditional love into our lives.

In the hustle of our busy lives, we tend to overlook our psychological needs. Especially with the demands of life—career, children, relationships, finances, or health issues—we lose sight of what is going on with our emotional needs. We may end up arguing about daily concerns that mask our underlying needs.

Conflict raises a red flag. It forces us to pay attention to what is missing or what needs to change. We may blame the conflict on our loved one. Instead, we need to ask ourselves what we are feeling and take responsibility for managing our own emotions. We all need love and want to be seen, heard, and understood, but it's our job to recognize these. As we clarify our needs, we can ask for what we want.

When desires remain hidden and unfulfilled, bitterness builds. If we don't have the insight to understand and express our needs, we may expect our partner to know what we need, especially if we are in a long-term relationship. We may feel angry for not receiving the kind of love we crave. The reality is that we can't read each other's minds.

Neglected needs build resentment and surface in indirect ways. For example, Alice's perpetual lateness masked her resentment that Rob didn't appreciate how hard she worked at home and on the job. She longed for appreciation, but didn't articulate it directly. Nagging was a cover for the desire to be heard. On the other hand, Rob felt neglected, disrespected, and unappreciated and looked to alcohol for comfort. He retaliated by blaming Alice's lateness for his need to drink. This eye for an eye attitude blinded them both to the real underlying issues.

How do we identify our needs when they may be buried? The majority of our relationship conflicts have nothing to do with differences of opinion about everyday events. If a couple argues about where to go on vacation, which restaurant to eat, or how to raise children, there are usually underlying issues. When we have different perspectives and we feel disrespected or devalued as individuals, arguments escalate. The everyday issues are often not what the fight is about. Conflict can unearth the hidden issues.

Deanna and Mark were married for eighteen years when they decided to divorce. They did not fight. Instead, they were coldly civil to each other. Over time, they felt like they had grown apart with nothing in common. When they came to Mari for mediation, they easily split up major high-value assets, such as three homes valued in the seven digits, expensive wine collections, and high dollar investments. Mari was surprised at how politely the couple collaborated, until they discussed the allocation of the Bavarian china and the photo albums. Suddenly, each became demanding. The photos were easily mediated by having them duplicated, with each sharing the cost. However, the Bavarian china caused a crisis. Shocked, Mari asked them what was so important about the china. They told her that it was purchased during their honeymoon in Bavaria. It became apparent that the china represented the love, passion, and companionship that they'd lost over the years once they stopped paying attention to each other. The china proved a pivotal point that created a catharsis and a new beginning. They tearfully told Mari of their idyllic romance in Europe and decided to put the divorce on hold. They then focused on sharing their feelings and their desire to satisfy one another's unmet needs.

Dr. Stella Ting-Toomey, a communication theorist, identified six unmet identity needs at the heart of most difficult conflicts.[3] They included the need for competence, autonomy, companionship, being valued, reliability, and integrity. Let's explore each one.

1. The need to be recognized as *competent*. We all wish to be seen as capable, intelligent, or skillful. If we feel demeaned or criticized by our partner, that need will cause a squabble. However, when our loved one acknowledges and compliments our contributions and talents, and acts in a supportive way, we feel fulfilled.

Harold owned a very successful business. He received considerable accolades from his associates and the community leaders. Meanwhile, his wife Amanda, who looked after the household and the four children, felt unappreciated and devalued. Though she provided for the comforts of the family, she felt neglected and incompetent. Over time, she became resentful and depressed. That prompted the couple to seek counseling from Leonard. He helped Harold to recognize Amanda's value in supporting him and taking great care of the family. He became more involved in caring

---

3   Ting-Toomey, Stella, and Chung, Leeva C., *Understanding Intercultural Communication*, New York: Oxford University Press, 2011.

for the children. That allowed Amanda to feel important. She eventually returned to school for a degree, and
the marriage flourished

2. The need for *autonomy*. We all yearn for a level of
self-reliance and independence. At the same time, we
want our emotional or physical boundaries respected. If
we feel smothered, controlled, or unable to make decisions for ourselves, we may fight for that right. However,
we need a balance between connecting as a couple and
being individuals, so we feel close enough to touch yet
far enough for the wind to blow between us.

Rachel was only twenty-two when she married Jared.
At forty, he was a very successful airline pilot. She ideal-
ized him while he supported her and the kids for twenty
years. He treated her as his little princess, showering
her with gifts, but controlling her every action. As she
matured, she wanted to be her own person and make
her own decisions. Yet Jared still wanted to be entirely in
control. When Rachel turned forty, she decided that she
had to end the marriage to be her own person. In mediation, Jared heard Rachel's concerns. He still wanted to
take care of his wife, but she wanted to be free.

3. The need for *companionship*. In a loving union, we
want quality time and connection. Companionship
involves conversations with a partner who listens and
acts like our friend. If our loved one does not seem
interested or treats us as unlikeable, we feel alienated,
rejected, or abandoned.

At times, couples will attempt therapy or end
up in divorce mediation, not because they fight, but
because they feel like strangers. They no longer

communicate or enjoy each other's company and have little companionship.

Dr. Marion Solomon, author of *Lean on Me*, states that a basic human need is to share distressing emotions with someone who will make us feel safe and supported. This builds trust.

When her sister suddenly became gravely ill while on vacation, Mari flew to Florida to support her sister and the family as they dealt with the heart-wrenching death and dying decisions. Mari felt the need to be strong and positive to assist her brother-in-law and the children through the dying and grieving process. At night, she tearfully called her husband, Lloyd, to lean on him for love and empathy. His comfort and sympathy sustained her through that very difficult time of loss.

4. The need to be *valued and held in a positive light.* We all want to be valued and appreciated for who we are. If a partner doesn't value us as attractive, we can feel unworthy and undesirable. Most of us want to be cherished and treasured and to hear words of praise.

When Joe and Annette first got together, they were very complimentary toward each other. They bragged to their friends about finding their soul mate. After a while, Joe began to criticize Ann about the way she looked and how she talked and laughed. In turn, she pointed out Joe's faults. The couple spiraled into a downward cycle of negativity as both felt devalued.

5. The need for *reliability.* We yearn for security and safety. We want to trust that our mate will be there for us and support us. If our partner lies, cheats, or betrays our love or confidences, we will feel insecure and unsafe.

When we trust that our partner will be there for good times and bad, during sickness and health, for financial crises and boom times, we can have a sense of security.

Francine was diagnosed with stage three cancer. Her devoted husband accompanied her to every doctor's appointment, cooked her nutritious meals, sat at her bedside in the hospital, and cheered her up with humorous cards and gifts. His support and love helped her in her recovery.

6. The need to be recognized as having *integrity*. Most of us want to live according to our values and seek the same from a partner. If we see that our loved one lacks integrity or continually acts dishonorably, we may feel ashamed and hypocritical. However, when we perceive our partner as having admirable values such as honesty, generosity, and faithfulness, we are reminded to emulate those values and live with integrity.

When John brought Ellen home to meet his family in Canada, he was shocked when she snubbed his parents. After he told her that he was hurt, Ellen admitted that she was disappointed that his parents came from a lower class. With that revelation, John's attitude changed. Not only were his parents offended, but also he felt disrespected by Ellen. Soon after, John broke off the engagement.

Our deepest hurts occur when our core identity is attacked. If we feel belittled or threatened, we may angrily lash out in defense or retreat into hurt and sadness. As a result, we may choose to fight, flee, or freeze. Some of us may respond overtly with hostility, suffer in silence, act in a passive-aggressive manner, or just walk out and leave.

Jane was a latchkey kid as a child. She learned that she had to take care of herself and could not depend on others. This created a need to control situations so she could get her needs met without having to depend on others. Unfortunately, her independence and control issues were a continual source of conflict with her spouse. Her micromanagement threatened her husband's need for autonomy.

As we become aware of our psychological needs and our emotional reactions, we can seek to satisfy ourselves without threatening the core needs of our loved one. When we and our partner support each other to clarify and meet needs, love in the relationship expands.

While talking about needs, we cannot overlook how gender differences affect our relationship. Biology, psychology, and culture cause men and women to think, perceive, communicate, problem solve, and negotiate differently. Both sexes share common needs of love and understanding, but the way we express those needs are unique.

Generally, women need deeper interconnection, a cooperative approach, empathy, open communication, and mutual support. Most men, traditionally, need independence, a feeling of achievement, healthy competition, a direct problem-solving approach, and a feeling of respect.

The combination of brain structure and hormonal differences offers a good explanation of why women and men see the world differently when in love. Young girls tend to use language and relationships when playing "house" or "school" and display cooperation, agreement, and support while avoiding conflict. Mutual understanding and closeness are highly valued in social situations. Boys, on the other hand, play in groups that are structured with rules and winners and losers. They are more comfortable with aggression and are encouraged to compete in sports. As boys become men, they value status, enjoy problem solving, and take more physical and personal risks.

The corpus callosum which connects the two hemispheres is different in men and women. This impacts the way both genders process information. It could be said that women have a four-lane highway between the two hemispheres, whereas men have a dirt road. This means that men may focus on one or two needs at a time, while women can express needs on multiple levels.

John Gray popularized the differences in gender in his *Men Are from Mars, Women are from Venus* series. He identified the primary love needs of women as needing to receive caring, understanding, respect, devotion, validation, and reassurance. On the other hand, men needed to receive trust, acceptance, appreciation, admiration, approval, and encouragement.[4]

When partners don't recognize the needs of the opposite sex, relationships suffer. If a woman tries to actively improve her partner—"What you need to do is..."—he may feel devalued and disrespected. When a man avoids listening to his partner and seeks to quickly fix any problem, she will likely feel misunderstood or unloved.

In the bedroom, men often need sexual intimacy to feel close, whereas women need to feel close before

---

4   Gray, John, *Men Are From Mars, Women Are From Venus: A Practical Guide for Improving Communication and Getting What You Want in Your Relationships*, New York: HarperCollins, 1992; pp. 133-134.

they have sex. According to John Gray, "A man experiences pleasure primarily as a release of sexual tension. A woman's pleasure corresponds to a gradual buildup of sexual tension."[5] When a couple is aware of their different needs for pleasure and work together to satisfy each other, they create more passion in their life.

When the needs of both genders are satisfied, we feel good; when they're not, we feel frustrated, mad, or sad. Unfortunately, we tend to expect our partner to understand and meet our needs, even if we, ourselves, are unaware of what we really want or desire. Conflict forces us to dig deeper to become more conscious of what we are feeling.

When our stomach is empty, it growls and alerts us of physical cravings, which then prompt us to recognize the need to eat. Taking action to get food eliminates our discomfort and brings relief and pleasure. When our body is hungry, it is in conflict. We can complain about being hungry, or we can be responsible and get food, enjoy our meal, and be grateful that our body's alert system prompted us to take action.

Conflict in relationships is also an alert system. It sends a signal that something needs to be addressed. We can ignore it or complain about it, but that does not turn the alarm off. When we listen to the alarm, we can discover our underlying feelings and take action to address our needs.

What action can you take when your conflict alarm goes off? A constructive option is to first ask yourself what you are feeling. When you identify an unmet need,

---

5   Gray, John, *Mars and Venus in the Bedroom: A Guide to Lasting Romance and Passion,* New York: Harper Perennial, 1997; p. 27.

such as the need to connect, you can communicate this in a calm, direct, and positive manner. However, if you say, "I need attention now," that may pressure your partner to hear it as a demand. Consider how what you say will be perceived. For example, you might say, "I missed you today and would love to have some special time together tonight. Are you available?"

We all have many layers of needs. They may not be easy to decipher in a stressful moment. We react to situations throughout the day. Emotional reactions call for attention. Anger and frustration take precedence before we can go below the surface and get to what's driving the emotions. If we can successfully negotiate our inner emotional mine field, we can effectively communicate about how we are feeling and express our genuine needs. The next step is to make positive requests so each person can be mutually satisfied.

As we wrote this chapter, we realized that despite all our training and years of experience working with couples, we struggled at times with clarifying our own needs in our individual lives and relationships. It takes time and introspection to reflect and decipher our emotions. Also, many of our emotions and needs are subconscious. So we clearly understand that figuring out underlying needs in a relationship takes effort and contemplation. The more we know what we need and want, the easier it is to give to ourselves and receive from our partner.

One of the remarkable benefits of a committed loving relationship is that it holds the possibility of a safe place where partners can satisfy their desires. However, finding the balance between looking after oneself and the needs of another can be challenging. If one person wants more space and the other needs to be close, the couple can brainstorm solutions to find a way to satisfy both closeness and independence. When a couple works through the differences, they learn to understand and appreciate each other in a new way.

Unearthing and clarifying how we are feeling and what we need helps to prevent escalating conflict. Raising our awareness as to what is going on within us not necessarily easy. Many of us have been taught as children to suppress underlying desires. We may have been told, "Be quiet," when we wanted to express excitement; "Get busy," when we wanted to play; or "Don't cry," when we wanted to show our pain. If we learned to accommodate our caregivers by short-circuiting our connection to feelings, sensations, thoughts, and desires, we would have difficulty as adults in accessing them.

If our needs for attention weren't met as a child, we would have adopted strategies to satisfy them. We may have placated, demanded, rebelled, seduced, or acted like a victim. These indirect strategies may help us get what we want but our partner may feel manipulated or controlled and resentful.

It takes awareness to dig beneath the surface and ask ourselves, moment by moment, "How do I feel and what do I really need or desire in this situation?" If you could ask yourself that question, you could avoid the misplaced anger that often turns into a struggle.

When Leonard works with couples, he often hears the comment, "If you loved me, you would know what I need." That sentiment is a setup for conflict. If you don't have a clue about what you need, chances are that your partner won't know either. Therefore, it's important that you express what you think and feel clearly.

When you ignore what's bothering you, resentment will expand beneath the surface like an iceberg. When the relation-ship barges into the iceberg, you will feel the exploding impact. The undeclared needs will cata-pult to the surface as an argument, as you shout, "You never understand me!"

Deciphering our physical sensations, thoughts, feel-ings, and behaviors enables us to discover what is missing in our lives. We can make requests, instead of demands, for what we want, to demonstrate mutual caring.

When you open the door to an intimate conversation about hearing each other's concerns, you bring more connection into the relationship. If you and your part-ner explore ways to satisfy one another's emotional and physical desires, you create a strong union and deep feelings of love.

Whenever you experience disagreements, look for the underlying core issues and needs that may be trig-gering the discord. Ask each other to consider what may be the deeper cause of the conflict. With patience and a nonjudgmental approach, you and your partner will become more comfortable being vulnerable with each other and discuss your feelings.

Now that we have analyzed various ways of under-standing needs and desires, we are ready to consider our personality styles and temperament, the subject of the next chapter.

FIGHTING FOR LOVE EXERCISES:

Imagine how you would feel and act if you felt understood, loved, and appreciated all the time by your partner.

1. Make a list of what you need in your love relationship; for example, affection, physical touch, understanding, time alone, words of appreciation, etc.

2. How are those needs being satisfied in your present situation?

3. What do you think your partner needs and how are those needs satisfied?

4. How could you and your partner make loving requests to mutually meet each other's desires? Here's a few examples:

   a. I'd like to discuss our finances.
   b. I'd love to have a fun date night where we don't discuss problems.

5. Ask your partner, "What could I do to I help you feel cherished?"

The most basic of all human needs is the need to understand and be understood. The best way to understand people is to listen to them.

– Ralph G. Nichols

"Remember what the marriage counselor said?
It only works if I <u>want</u> to change!"

CHAPTER 4

Who Am I? Who Are You?

Life is more amusing, more interesting, and more of a daily adventure than it could possibly be if everyone were alike.

— Isabel Briggs Myers

Lindsay was outgoing and personable. She enjoyed having company over for parties and dinner. Her fiancé Alan was more reserved and socially awkward. He was attracted to Lindsay's beauty, brains, and the fact that she was well liked by everyone she met. He believed she would be a great partner in life and would support his corporate career advancement. Lindsay was attracted to Alan's good looks, his attentiveness to her, his motivation to get ahead, and his logical mind. This power couple appeared perfect for each other—until their styles clashed after they started living together.

Alan was uncomfortable when Lindsay made the rounds at parties, leaving him to fend for himself. She couldn't understand why he didn't join in, especially since he wanted to climb the corporate ladder. At the end of an evening of socializing, Alan's distant cool approach froze Lindsay's passion. Every time they went out socially, they ended up quarreling. Both felt judged and disconnected. They clearly didn't understand or appreciate each other's personality style.

How does personality style and temperament cause us to engage in conflict?

We each tend to have a style or a temperament that reveals itself, even as early as when we are little children. Our unique character shows up in our individual thought patterns, emotions, and behaviors. As we grow up and experience life, we develop distinctive personality and coping strategies to survive and thrive. This helps us get what we want when we want it.

Our styles are also affected by our emotional intelligence, which comprises our level of self-awareness, our ability to manage ourselves, and the way we relate to others. While our personality style tends to remain the same, we can reduce conflict by learning the skills of emotional intelligence to cooperate with our partner given his/her style and whether it meshes or clashes with our way of relating.

Some of us appear to be born leaders, while others may be more reserved, yet are great supporters. We may be detail oriented, organized, and stick to rules and strict budgets. We may be with someone who is laid back or spontaneous about spending and planning. Our partner could be someone who enjoys a spirited argument or who likes to logically analyze a problem, while we may want to collaborate and keep the peace at all costs to avoid an argument. One may feel it's important to stick to principles and be right no matter what, and the other may value flexibility and change and would rather be happy than right.

No matter what our style, each of us has grown up with ways of thinking and behaving that have met our needs in previous situations. We, therefore, may continue to act in certain ways, oblivious to how our styles affect our loved ones. We each have positive personality characteristics that can be appreciated. However, our styles may collide with our loved one's temperament. When our ways of approaching life are incongruent with our partner's mode, we may end up in major disputes. Recognizing our differences helps us see how we are perceived. We can then accommodate each other.

When we first meet someone who we find attractive, we are excited to spend time together. We enjoy learning about each other and are thrilled when we experience similar interests. We become smitten. Our connection may be so intense that we believe we have found our soul mate. Even though we may share similar ideals and goals and seem to be in sync, after a while, we will discover that we are each different. Opposites attract, so we can learn from each other. If one of us tends to be passive, we may be attracted to an outgoing and energetic partner to help us expand socially. If one of us is a strong leader, we may be attracted to a supportive partner who wishes to follow and be a caring sidekick.

Most romantic movies have two individuals who end up on an idealistic quest to find what is missing in themselves to create balance in their lives. A love interest brings two people together so they can complete their lives. Of course, any good romance has drama and conflict as the couple wrestle to see how the pieces fit together.

We come together in relationships to discover ourselves, evolve, and learn new perspectives. Engaging with a lover gives us an opportunity to mature and experience new ways of seeing the world. However, after the infatuation fades, the very traits that originally attracted and drew us to each other can later seem like flaws that we want our partner to eliminate. That is when struggles begin. After a while, we come to the conclusion that we must change our partner to be more like us, and if we accomplish that, we will be happy and live happily ever after. Unfortunately, when we believe the other should change, the battle begins.

Glen and Madeline went to purchase a new bed. Glen preferred a soft mattress while Madeline wanted a firm one. Each had their own preferences and argued the merits of their case. Clearly, one's comfort translated into the other's discomfort. The same often happens in relationships with each fighting for her or his own cause. The solution can be as simple as accepting one another's style. In Glen and Madeline's case, they purchased twin mattresses, each for their own comfort, and joined them together.

Exploring the similarities and differences of our own style with that of our partner enables us to gain a clearer understanding of how our approach to life positively or negatively impacts our relationship. When we see our differences as interesting traits that expand our consciousness, instead of finding fault, we show each other mutual respect and positive acknowledgment. Valuing our partner's strengths and practicing patience with their weaknesses creates an environment of appreciation that nurtures love.

No one personality style is better than another, though we may get along better with certain personality types. We grow from being open to each other's uniqueness. Understanding and acceptance are the keys that help us satisfy each other's needs.

Acceptance and Adjustments to Stylistic Differences Lead to Harmony

When there is conflict, it is easy to blame our partner for having a particular personality trait. If we accuse our loved one of being too controlling or having a manipulative style, or being too lazy or too anything, we become judgmental. No one wants to be judged. Focusing on what we don't like about our partner's personality polarizes the relationship. Criticism or condemnation make us feel indignant, and cause us to counterattack, rebel, or bury feelings with resentment.

In the scenario at the beginning of this chapter, Lindsay was an extrovert while Alan was an introvert. When she felt attacked for her outgoing nature, she rebelled against his criticism. Whenever they went to social events, she wanted to spend more time away from him. Lindsay interpreted Alan's introversion as being non-communicative and aloof. Without understanding her need to connect, Alan viewed Lindsay as inconsiderate and overbearing. Although they weren't going to change each other's basic natures, they could expand their perspective, refrain from criticizing, and understand each other's underlying needs. They would honor each other's differences if they communicated about what was going on inside of them.

To illustrate, Lindsay could ask Alan how he was feeling at an event and what he needed from her so he would feel more comfortable. She could respect Alan's desire that she spend more time with him and bring him into conversations with others. Rather than leaving him with people he didn't know, Lindsay could introduce Alan to people who have similar interests so he could engage more easily. She could hold his hand and demonstrate social skills in various conversations.

Alan could appreciate Lindsay's outgoing nature and stretch himself by reaching out to others. He could expand his own social network to include like-minded individuals so he's not so dependent on Lindsay. Alan might decide not to attend certain events during which Lindsay was required to network. That way he could take the time to do things he would rather do by himself or with his own friends. Accepting one another's personality differences would be an ongoing process of their growth as a couple.

As lovers recognize that each other's patterns are as valid as their own, they allow themselves to be influenced by the best of those characteristics and can even replicate them. For example, Mari's husband Lloyd, who is more laid back, has shown her how to slow down and go with the flow. Mari, on the other hand, has influenced Lloyd at times to adopt her tendency to passionately move forward with projects. To avoid polarizing, they try to accommodate each other while still being themselves.

Couples who enjoy long-term marriages respect and trust each other. They appreciate one another for who they are without trying to change them. Of course, this involves communication about what does and does not work for them. Acting as mirrors for each other, they help each other see a different perspective. With a deeper understanding of each other's concerns and feelings, each can choose to change his or her own behavior as an act of love.

Who Are You?

There are numerous personality assessment instruments to help you analyze who you are. You can find many reputable personality tests online, some for free. Here are a few:

- DISC (www.onlinediscprofile.com)

- Myers-Briggs Indicator (www.myersbriggs.org)

- The Keirsey Temperament Sorter (www.keirsey.com)

- Enneagram (www.enneagraminstitute.com)

Of the various categories of personality types, some assessments are quite complicated, providing up to sixteen or more types of personalities. These tests offer unique ways of analyzing yourself. One of the least complicated is DISC. It has four main categories with a variety of combinations of the four styles: Dominant, Influencer, Steady, and Conscientious.

Dr. William Marston developed the DISC model at Columbia University in the 1920s, and later, Dr. John Geier of the University of Minnesota updated

Marston's research and created a personality profile to help individuals discover their own DISC styles. Wiley Publishing now owns these DISC tests and provides you the opportunity to discover your personality style online. Although most of us fall predominately into one category, we may be a mixture of other styles. Additionally, some circumstances may require that we take on a particular approach.

One who is usually a supporter or a Steady will need at times to take on a Dominant approach as a parent or when addressing a crisis. A person who normally has a Conscientious, introverted style may need to display characteristics of an outgoing Influencer when trying to persuade others. For those who like to entertain and influence others, they will need a less socially conscious approach when planning a detailed project.

When you are aware of your own hot buttons and those that offend your partner, you can deflect conflict situations and engage in loving, problem-solving approaches that meet your partner's style. For example, if your partner is a dominant, he or she will want to take the lead in a discussion. You can be supportive and respectful and listen attentively.

Consider below which of these categories sounds most like you, then consider which of these categories appears to be most like your loved one. Remember, all styles have their positive attributes and advantages in some situations and weaknesses in others. For purposes of ease, we have adapted the DISC approach with our own categories to give you and your partner a simple assessment tool to transform possible conflict into collaboration.

The acronym **CASE** will help you remember four major styles that you and your partner may demonstrate.

C — Commander (one who is dominant and results oriented)

A — Analyzer (one who exhibits conscientiousness and emphasizes accuracy)

S — Supporter (one who exhibits steadiness and emphasizes cooperation)

E — Engager (one who influences and emphasizes relationships)

Are you or your partner a Commander type?

Some strong leaders include: General Patton; Donald Trump; Hillary Clinton; and Margaret Thatcher.

In a love relationship do you or your partner need to:

Y or N: Assume authority and control in the relationship or family

Y or N: Have others show great respect

Y or N: Assume the ultimate authority to make the decisions

Y or N: Prefer to be seen as a leader

Y or N: Address challenges head-on and be the major problem solver

Y or N: Make quick decisions and move quickly

Y or N: Be informed of facts, not emotions

Y or N: Know *what* rather than *why* something is happening

Y or N: Deliberate logically and quickly

Y or N: Demand freedom from control from your partner

What are the positive attributes of the Commanding Style in a love relationship?

This leader type of personality gets things done quickly and can take charge when his/her partner is ambivalent, fearful, or needs direction or leadership. When there is an emotionally trying situation, this person can quickly take charge and manage a stressful or dangerous situation. When challenges arise, the Commander uses reasoned caution and logical thinking to make decisions. This style works well with a supportive partner who doesn't butt heads. As a strong leader, she or he is usually successful in business.

When you need a good problem solver to think on his/her feet efficiently and quickly, this type gets the job done. Being confident and self-assured, this personality speaks directly so you know the issues quickly.

How would a Commanding type react when engaged in conflict?

Commanders are often very competitive in conflict. In a dispute, you may feel bruised and beaten. During an argument, this person may become domineering, controlling, intimidating, and even may seem like a bully. If you interrupt this personality, it may result in rage. He/she may be willing to fight tooth and nail to prove he or she is right. This style may try to pressure a partner to accept his/her reasoning with warnings or threats. Commanders will use logical arguments to show that you are wrong and may belittle your emotions. In conflict, this type of approach wants you to do what he or she wants without an argument. When the pressure is on, he/she would rather be right than happy and may do whatever they want without collaboration. If you win a dispute, this will make the Commander type angry and she/he may look for ways to retaliate and escalate conflict.

George was much older than Lisa when they married. She looked up to him to take care of her. He made a good living and supported her in a nice house, but he controlled all the finances, the children, and every move she made. He was a Commander, and she was a Supporter. It worked for a while, until she could no longer express herself without criticism. She felt downtrodden and finally left him. The pain that she kept inside for years destroyed her love for George.

Strategies to manage conflict with a Commander

If the Commander style sounds like you or your partner, be mindful of what this personality style needs. The following approach will help the Commander in the relationship feel more in control and respected, yet allow for the dignity of the Commander's partner without a need to fight:

- Don't try to prove the Commander is wrong. Use a logical approach to express your needs or concerns. Talk about the pros and cons of what you both are proposing, and show how the Commander will get his or her needs meet.

- Research facts before presenting a suggestion and use a neutral tone of voice, keeping the emotions at bay. Present your desires in a way that honors your loved one and demonstrates your acknowledgment of his/her positive attributes. Let him or her know that you will accommodate, while still respecting your own desires and boundaries.

- Give direct answers when asked questions about your concerns. If you are indirect, it will be perceived by the Commander as manipulative and disingenuous.

- Never appear overpowering or condescending. Repeat back what was said to you to show your partner that you value his/her opinion. Ask what she or he thinks will be a workable solution. Avoid asking questions that require specific details about how something should be resolved.

- Allow your partner to have the last word, after you come up with a resolution that you are comfortable agreeing to follow. Thank him/her for his advice and input even if you gave him the solution.

- Don't acquiesce to all that she/he wants, but respect his style and authority to get what you need and desire. If he/she says it's "my way or the highway," tell him or her that you want to resolve things in a way that retains dignity for both. In some situations, you might want to take the highway.

- Show your partner respect and admiration. He or she will respond and give you the same.

The challenge for this driven personality style is to learn to compromise, relax, let go, collaborate, and have more fun.

Are you or your partner an Analyzer type?

Examples of the Analyzer personality are: Albert Einstein; Jackie Kennedy Onassis; Diane Sawyer; Colombo; and Bill Gates.

In a love relationship, do you or your partner need:

Y or N: An analytical approach to discussions

Y or N: Details about everything that happens

Y or N: A step-by-step methodology

Y or N: A systematic approach to the relationship

Y or N: A conservative approach to clothing and environment

Y or N: Socializing in small versus large groups

Y or N: Distance and controlled communication without emotions

Y or N: An opportunity to ask "why" questions to get detailed answers

Y or N: Recognition for accomplishments

What are the positive attributes of the Analyzer style in a love relationship?

If you or your partner is an Analyzer, display diplomacy, courtesy, and restraint. This conservative personality type is often detail oriented, careful, meticulous, and cautious. He/she wants to do a job as best as possible and will strive for perfectionism. As a lover, he/she will analyze what is wrong and do whatever is needed to make the relationship work. This personality sets high standards for self and others, but tries not to offend others. Although not comfortable demonstrating much emotion, underneath the exterior, he or she can be very sensitive and caring. An Analyzer wants to be his or her own person, independent, yet very loyal when appreciated.

How may an Analyzer react when engaged in conflict?

In the midst of conflict, this style tends to be evasive and avoid meaningful problem solving and especially conflict. She or he may ask you to just let go of a dispute, and put it under the rug. Under stress, Analyzers may become rigid, stubborn, rebellious, defiant, offensive, and sarcastic. When pressured, this style may become tactless and self-righteous and close off meaningful discussions, even walk out the door. This person may circumvent when you are in an argument and turn the tables on you with blame or guilt. Instead of listening to his/her partner in an angry situation, he or she can become very opinionated and unreasonable. This personality may need time to reflect and analyze before opening up.

Jane, an accountant, was very conscientious. She would bring home her work at night and not even talk to her husband or kids until bedtime. Mike would try to talk to her about their lack of communication, but she would blame him that she had to work so hard. Jane's sharp tongue demoralized Mike. For the sake of their kids, they finally sought counseling. Jane learned to manage her anger and put up a *do not disturb* sign when she needed to work. Mike learned to make appointment times for communicating and romance.

Strategies to manage conflict with an Analyzer

- Clarify your expectations in the conversation and speak calmly. Explain concerns carefully, making sure not to attack or surprise your mate.

- Be precise and support your ideas with accurate data without infusing emotion.

- Demonstrate to your loved one that it's safe to open up with feelings and intimacy.

- Show respect and appreciation for his/her analysis and methodical approach. Be a good listener and take your time. Don't jump into a heavy relationship discussion without giving your partner a heads-up to prepare. Make a time to talk when there is little stress.

- Think through what you want before you engage in a challenging discussion. Present the pros and cons of your reasoning. Rather than being direct and skipping the prelude, method-ically give a step-by-step approach, easing into a discussion about a difficult issue.

- When addressing problems, use facts from both of your perspectives and compromise as much as possible. Acknowledge and com-pliment the analytical approach and his/her reasoning.

- Give your loved one a chance to demonstrate how his/her reasoned approach to resolving the conflict situation is effective.

- Set up clear goals and a well-structured conser-vative approach to addressing concerns.

- Encourage your partner not to run from con-flict, but to calmly use a systematic approach such as solutioneering, outlined in Chapter 10.

The challenge for the Analyzer is to be more engaging, explore emotions, and be open to new perspectives.

Are you or your partner a Supporter personality type?

Some examples of Supporters include: Mother Teresa; Melinda Gates; Michael J Fox; and Laura Bush.

In a relationship, do you or your partner need:

Y or N: Security and trust in your love connection

Y or N: Time to adjust to changes

Y or N: Appreciation and compliments

Y or N: Harmony and minimal conflict

Y or N: Displays of loyalty

Y or N: Recognition of self-worth

Y or N: Structured negotiations

Y or N: Patience in drawing out concerns

Y or N: A feeling of being helpful supportive

Y or N: Sincerity and warmth

Y or N: Predictable routines

What are the positive attributes of the Supporter style in a love relationship?

A Supporter can be loyal, predictable, and stable. He or she creates a harmonious and positive ambiance. A good listener, a person with this tendency can calm others down and be very likable and helpful. This style is often outgoing, gregarious, eager, and enthusiastic. However, they may be happy to support behind the scenes. Their optimism is contagious. This helps the relationship to get through tough times. Known for their patience, they buoy up their partner. In a loving relationship, the nurturing aspect of this style helps to glue the intimate connection in an amiable and soothing manner.

How does a Supporter react in conflict?

This personality style is very conflict-adverse, so in a challenging situation, the Supporter may be very accommodating and give in, but then become resentful later. By not expressing his/her concerns, he or she may agree but not get needs met. If that is the case, they may appear passive aggressive and hide their anger. At that point, he/she may become very critical, blaming, and abrupt. Normally optimistic, this style becomes negative, complacent, and frustrated under pressure. His/her usual friendly nature may turn negative with discontent. Rather than deal with an issue when it arises, this personality runs away from arguments and quickly disengages. You may find him or her impetuous and spontaneous in a negative situation.

Jeff was a CEO of his own company and a gregarious leader. When he met Lynn, she was enthralled with his power and charisma. He told her he would always take care of her. He showered her with love and affection until the kids were born. Then he focused on work and the kids. At first, she would hide her anger and become resentful. This caused her to become passive aggressive. When Jeff confronted her, she would leave with the kids and visit her mother. When she couldn't get the attention and love she needed, she asked her husband for a divorce. In mediation, the couple recognized their different styles and worked on accommodating one another.

Strategies to manage conflict with a Supporter

- Use a gentle approach when handling conflict. Speak slowly and calmly. During a flare-up, wait for your partner to regain composure.

- Show sincerity and gentleness with difficult challenges.

- Set up a relaxed, trusting atmosphere in which to bring up issues. Since this style may be quite passive, patiently encourage engagement with an optimistic approach that everything will work out.

- Value your partner and let him or her know you need the support. Appreciate his/her harmonious approach.

- Be loving and warm and optimistic.

- Make her/him feel secure and safe by displaying attention and loyalty.

- Give him/her time to adjust to changes in routine.

The challenge of a Supporter is to create inner security so they can gently confront issues that bother them and not bottle up emotions.

Are you or your partner an Engager personality type?

Some examples of this personality type are Bill Clinton, Kate Hudson, Steve Martin, and Oprah Winfrey.
In a relationship do you need:

Y or N: Freedom to talk and share ideas

Y or N: Time for your independence

Y or N: A positive environment

Y or N: Openness and trust

Y or N: Fun and excitement

Y or N: Opportunities to be creative

Y or N: Occasions to socialize with friends

Y or N: Engagement and entertainment

Y or N: Permission to express emotions and feelings freely

Y or N: A trusting atmosphere

What are the positive attributes of the Engager style in a love relationship?

This personality style is generally optimistic and won't rain on your sunshine. He or she brings fun, friendship, and sociability to the relationship. Your lover will be able to persuade and convince you to connect and may convince you to do things you may not ordinarily be willing to do. She/he is enthusiastic about life and can charm you. Often generous with time, talent, and treasure, she or he will inspire and cheer you up when feeling down. The Engager's trusting nature builds connection easily. However, he/she may be too trusting at times. This style loves the freedom to be with friends and not feel smothered. Spontaneous, fun-loving, and ready to entertain, this partner is charismatic with a family, and friends,

How does an Engager manage conflict?

This style can be quite emotional, dramatic, and intense in conflict. As a socializer, the Engager will try to bring everyone together and compromise. At his/her best, the Engager will be a collaborator and get his or her partner to open up and share their views and feelings to work out an agreement that addresses each other's needs. She/he doesn't beat around the bush and is very direct, which may come off as aggressive. The Engager is persistent and will usually not give up until the problem is solved. Under pressure, this style can become suspicious and blunt. Negativity debilitates this type of person. Raining on his/her sunshine will prolong the conflict.

Arnie was loved by everyone. He was friendly and always brought life to any situation. Angie, a very beautiful artist, was reserved and didn't feel comfortable expressing her feelings. When Arnie prodded Angie to talk when she was upset, she would clam up. This frustrated Arnie to the point where he would become more verbally aggressive. Not surprisingly, this pushed Angie deeper into her shell.

Strategies to manage conflict with an Engager

- Allow your partner to share his/her feelings.

- Be cautious of offending this person, for he or she will use a sharp tongue to criticize you to escalate the conflict.

- Be open with your feelings, but don't confront harshly. An attack will push his/her buttons and unleash a flood of emotions.

- Smile and add levity, but not sarcasm. Be positive about finding a solution. Avoid bringing your partner down with negativity or pessimism.

- Ask open-ended questions about concerns and be respectful and grateful for your partner's sincere answers. Ask your partner to suggest solutions.

- Be trustworthy and don't dodge the truth to avoid a confrontation. That will backfire and you may have a difficult time regaining trust.

- Open up to your loved one and focus on how great it will be to resolve the issues and make up.

- Give your partner the freedom to be sociable and gregarious, and you will have a loyal and fun lover.

The challenge for an Engager is to become more comfortable with negative interactions, not take things personally, and focus on problem solving.

Vive la différence and Compatibility

We are often a blend of two or three of these styles. Actually, we have the capacity to adopt any one of these styles, depending on the circumstances and roles. If we have young children, we need to act like Commanders, especially when there is danger. If we want to persuade and motivate, we can utilize the attributes of the Engager. When our partner is hurting or ill, we need to take on the role of Supporter. If we have to tackle a financial issue, we want to access that part of us that is the Analyzer.

When considering compatibility, if we are a Commander type, we may find that the Supporter will help us reach our goals and not compete with us as much as an Engager, who is a strong leader as well. If we have Analyzer tendencies, we may feel more comfortable with a Commander who will appreciate and expect perfection and bottom line results. If we have Engager tendencies, we will enjoy the social scene and appreciate the Supporter who will be there to support our adventures. An Analyzer can help the Engager be grounded and take care of things that need to get done. The Supporter will benefit greatly from the Engager who will be positive and provide an encouraging approach that the Supporter relishes.

No matter our personality style, we can grow from our relationship with a lover who has a different approach to life. Once we understand each other's styles, we can communicate more consciously and appreciate our partner's unique personality. Conflict of styles can then be turned more easily into intimacy.

FIGHTING FOR LOVE EXERCISES:

1. After looking at the lists of the personality categories, what is your main style?

2. What is your partner's dominant style?

3. Consider a recent argument. What approach did you use? How might you have handled it differently, considering your partner's style?

4. Given your style, how might you let your partner know what you need to de-escalate conflict and create more intimacy?

"My last boyfriend said I'm a control freak.
Do you think I'm a control freak? If so, say yes."

CHAPTER 5

Stop the Destructive Patterns

You never change things by fighting the existing reality. To change something, build a new model that makes the existing model obsolete.

— Buckminster Fuller

Paul woke up at five in the morning, an hour before he had to get ready for work. He felt a passionate urge to make love to Cathy. She slept soundly next to him. He yearned to connect with his wife, for it had been awhile since they'd had sex. They both led busy careers, while also rearing two children. Their hectic schedules and the stress hindered intimate encounters.

Paul lay awake, agitated and tense. Should he disturb Cathy or should he let her sleep? He often felt this dilemma in the morning. When he and Cathy began their courtship, they both were equally hungry for one another, any time of day. Over the years, however, with the strain of full-time jobs, finances, and child rearing, the fire diminished, like logs growing cold in a fireplace.

Paul was an energetic early riser. Cathy stayed up late, preferring to sleep until the alarm shook her awake. Their body rhythms weren't in sync, a cause of conflict.

The more she rebuffed him, the more he suppressed his desire. He wanted to avoid feeling rejected. Yet, this morning, he wondered if it might be different, that his wife would be in the mood.

He slowly reached out to stroke her back. Her body stirred, then tensed. Occasionally, that meant she wanted him; most often, it meant she wanted to be left alone. He moved his hand across her back toward her chest. If only Cathy would wake up and oblige.

Cathy felt Paul's hand touch her skin. She stiffened her body again. A flood of resentment washed over her body. How many times had she told her husband that she preferred evenings for sex? Yet he persisted. She loved him, but wished he would be less selfish and more sensitive to her needs.

She kept her back to him, hoping he would get the message. When his hand stroked her thighs, she bristled. Another task on a list-filled day. She mentally added, "Have sex with Paul." Could she fit it in?

If she satisfied him, she wouldn't have to worry about finding time later. She resented that her own needs were being neglected. She felt guilty, believing a woman should be available for her man. After all, he was a good father and hard worker, and he needed stress relief. She sighed at the internal conflict. She had deprived Paul of sex on many mornings. On those days, he would leave for work grumpy and then come home in a dreadful mood.

The couple had stopped talking about their lack of intimacy because it usually ended up in an argument.

She didn't want to endure another strained day. She had plenty on her plate, the way it was.

As Paul continued to stroke her thighs, Cathy made a decision. She turned over and faced him. "I have to get up soon. Make it quick."

Rather than starting the day with an intimate connection, Paul and Cathy both experienced resentment. While the bedroom is often considered a sanctuary for love and rest, it can also become a battleground for couples to replay negative patterns.

Paul and Cathy were caught in a repetitive pattern where neither felt satisfied. Paul hoped the morning lovemaking would satisfy his physical needs and build a stronger bond with his wife. Yet his fear of rejection was reinforced by Cathy, who saw his early morning desire as an inconsiderate act that would sap her energy. Cathy's desire for intimacy and connection was strong, but she needed it at a time when she could relax and enjoy her husband's touch. Lovemaking for her was not just a quickie stress reliever. Feeling guilty and pressured, she resentfully agreed, but didn't feel respected or cherished. The mutual cycle of resentment created a negative pattern for them.

Clearly, this couple needed to break their pattern of frustration. Otherwise, their resentment and anger would extinguish the flames of love and passion. A constructive dialogue would shift the energy and offer an opportunity for intimacy.

Cathy: *I have to get up soon. I'm feeling pressure to acquiesce, but I do want to make love with you.*

Paul: *Honey, I miss being close to you. When can we make time for ourselves?*

Cathy: *Tonight, let's put the kids to bed early and turn off the TV. I'll wear your favorite Victoria Secret's outfit. We can have fun.*

Paul: *Can't wait!*

A heartfelt conversation takes time and skills to think before we speak. If we sift out any blame and explain what we are feeling, we create an opportunity to move past our fears of an argument to a genuine discussion about what we desire.

With careers, finances, and children requiring attention, Paul and Cathy could easily neglect their relationship. The immediate need to resolve problems was often postponed till later, after the tasks of the day had been accomplished. Oftentimes, those challenging situations never got revisited or resolved because it was considered too stressful at the end of the day. Issues left unresolved led to resentment.

An honest conversation without blame or guilt would open the door to intimacy and a more passionate relationship. The challenge for the couple was to create the space to share feelings when neither was stressed or pressed for time.

Paul and Cathy analyzed their recurring conflict later when they had time to think it through in counseling. With new tools, they could stop the negative patterns and create new ways of relating. They could see how they pushed each other's buttons and how they created a cyclical pattern that evolved over time. When they had a dialogue, they told each other:

Paul: *I look forward to making love with you. I can focus on you and forget about the pressures at work.*

Cathy: *I feel the same way. Let's make time this evening.*

Paul: *When I reach out to you in the morning and you tense up, I feel rejected. As a kid, I felt rejection by my parents. They were too busy for me. When I'm upset with you, I'm less sensitive to your needs.*

Cathy: *I feel bad that you feel rejected because I love you. I don't want to cause you to feel that way. I am under a lot of pressure to get to work in the morning.*

Paul: *I know you're under a lot of stress, but we need some loving time.*

Cathy: *When you coax me to make love in the morning and I have to go to work, I feel guilty. I want to be loving but feel resentful when you don't think of me.*

Paul: *I don't want you to resent me.*

Cathy: *I guess my anger goes back to when I was a kid. I was forced to make everyone happy before I could do what I wanted. I don't want to neglect my needs or yours.*

Paul: *So let's find a time that works for both of us to make love more often.*

Patterns are often passed down from generation to generation, without us realizing it. This is demonstrated in the story about a young girl who approached her mother while she was preparing breakfast. "Why do you cut bacon into tiny strips?" asked the daughter. The mother responded emphatically, "That's what my mother taught me." When the grandmother visited the family later in the week, the young girl asked her why bacon was cut into tiny strips. "I don't know," answered the grandmother. "That's what my mother taught me." As it so happened, the great-grandmother was still alive. When the girl next visited her, she questioned her about the bacon. The aged woman scratched her puzzled face and thought for a while. Then the light bulb went on. "Honey, we were so poor we could only afford a small frying pan."

The above example demonstrates an unconscious pattern. By the time we are six years old, we've received over 50,000 hours of programming. That unconscious programming established a network of neural pathways in the brain. Those programs influenced our choice of partners. Two people attracted to one another, in effect, hooked into each other's programs.

If Irene had parents who were too busy to make her feel special, she might be attracted to a busy man. He may initially shower her with affection and love, which is what she craves, but over time, will return to his busy lifestyle. This would trigger Irene's wound of neglect and create conflict. However, if Irene recognized that she was triggered by her childhood wound, she could take steps toward healing. Her partner could offer her an opportunity to express her needs and receive the love she desires.

Edgar received the message from his parents that he wasn't good enough. He was attracted to a woman who made him feel special. However, over time, his childhood programming continually scanned for incidents by his partner, which reinforced the message that he wasn't good enough. In essence, Edgar replayed the old messages until they became a self-fulfilling prophecy He later complained that his partner didn't value him. When he recognized his pattern, he adopted the tools in this book to feel good about himself.

Patterns unconsciously regulate our thoughts, feelings, and behaviors. Healthy patterns, such as eating together as a family, having a positive work ethic, and sharing appreciation, maintain constancy, strengthen relationships, and foster loving traditions. However, some of the established coping patterns that we learned don't fulfill our present needs and instead harm relationships. These can be addictive behaviors, such as workaholism, blaming, withdrawing, shutting down, etc.

Unconscious patterns continue in relationships until we intentionally alter them. It's easier to spot the annoying habits of our partner and to quickly recommend how he or she should change, such as *correctly* hanging the toilet roll or placing the silverware in the dishwasher the *right* way. If our partner perceives feedback as petty, blaming, critical, or controlling, it will backfire. Our loved one may rebelliously resist what we would like them to do. It's far better to ask for what we want rather than complain about what we don't want.

Observe recurring patterns

In order to reinforce positive patterns and rid yourself of the negative ones, you must first observe your recurring patterns. You can ask yourself, "What do I do or say that provokes a negative reaction from my partner?" After you list those scenarios, ask yourself, "What does my loved one do or say that pushes my buttons?" Do you encourage my partner's positive communication or shut it down?

These questions help you become more self-aware and recognize your own unique styles of managing conflict. Whether you fight back or cringe at the thought of disagreements and withdraw, conflict management styles are forged in childhood and continue until you see how they no longer serve you and consciously change them.

Amanda was taught as a child that conflict could lead to violence, as it did with her parents. She became hyper-vigilant about any disagreement and withdrew as soon as she felt tension. The same pattern continued with her husband, fearing that arguments would lead to violence. As a result, she avoided discussing difficult issues and neglected her own needs. Once she recognized this fear and how it related to the past, she worked on a communication style that did not blame or criticize. One of the gifts that conflict with her husband offered was the opportunity to practice alternative ways to express herself in a safe environment.

Each of us brings into our current relationships the behavioral patterns from our family of origin and previous relationships. For example, Ursula nagged her partner, Brad, about cleaning up after himself, in the hopes that he would listen to her and help out with chores. Brad felt harassed and responded by withdrawing, hoping that Ursula would stop talking. His withdrawal, however, triggered her feelings of rejection, and she persisted with the nagging, believing she would eventually be heard. The more she nagged, the more withdrawn and uncommunicative he became.

This continued for some time until Brad screamed, "Shut up!" Ursula, feeling fearful and rejected, broke down into tears. Both retreated into their own respective corners. The cycle continued to be repeated until one of them altered the pattern with a new approach.

Often, a couple can't seem to break the pattern until they contact a therapist or mediator who can point out what is happening. Recognizing that conflict is a call to fight for love, couples can focus on and revise the way they communicate. A more productive habit of listening and understanding, without nagging, yelling, blaming, criticizing, or accusing, helps us all get the love we deserve.

It takes conscious awareness to recognize patterns that don't serve us. Reliving the same type of conflicts over and over is crazy-making. Insanity is doing the same thing repeatedly and expecting a different result. We unconsciously choose loved ones who recreate patterns with us so that we can confront those underlying wounds from the past and move beyond them. If we don't address those issues with a current partner, they will surface in the next relationship. Conflict forces us to recognize the destructive patterns and change. If we ignore the patterns, we will remain stuck in the repeating cycle.

Altering unhealthy patterns is like learning a new skill, such as driving a car. When we get behind the wheel for the first time, we start out unskilled. We don't know what we don't know until a driver honks at us or the driving instructor screams. Suddenly, we become aware of a problem with our driving. We then create new habits by practicing the new behaviors to become more a competent driver. If we don't manage our driving differently, we will get stopped by a police officer or end up in an accident.

This learning analogy is similar to what happen in our relationships. After the infatuation stage, we become oblivious to our behaviors and their impact on our partner. Conflict is an alarm that forces us to become aware of problems. When we recognize our patterns, we can make a decision to become skillful lovers.

To identify your own patterns, think of a recent or recurring conflict and answer these questions:

- What happened to trigger the conflict?

- How were your buttons pushed?

- Did you respond by attacking, defending, withdrawing, or dismissing or denying the feeling, or did you express your perspective and needs clearly?

- Does your response remind you of a time when you were a child or in a past relationship?

- Now fill in the blanks to these sentences:

  c. When my partner says or does

     _____

  d. I feel

     _____

  e. I react by saying or doing

     _____

  f. Then my partner says or does

     _____

Here are some examples:

Sandy: *When my husband continues to watch TV when I try to talk to him about the kids, I feel disrespected. I react in an angry manner and demand that he listens to me. Then he gets angry and tells me to get off his back.*

Here's an alternative way to stop the pattern:

Sandy: *If my husband is watching TV, I tell him that I'd love to talk to him about the kids. When can we do this?*

Joel: *When my wife complains that I spend too much money, I feel criticized and complain that she needs to cut her expenses. She walks out of the room.*

An alternative approach:

Joel: *When my wife complains that I spend too much money, I tell her, "I know you are worried about paying bills. Let's set a time later tonight to see how we can make our finances work."*

Since the first step to change is awareness, let's explore the typical reactive behavioral patterns regarding conflict. When we encounter disagreements, we have three choices: we can avoid; engage in an argument; or resolve the issues.

Conflict Avoiders

They tend to withdraw, ignore, or deny problems, hoping they will go away. For them, disagreements are emotionally upsetting, believing they could lead to separation, angry outbursts, or even violence. If they were brought up in a household where arguments were commonplace, they may be terrified of reenactments.

On the other hand, if their parents taught them never to disagree with them, they may have learned passive aggressive behaviors whenever conflict arose. Some common examples of conflict avoiders include:

A. *Placating.* These individuals work hard at acting nice, pleasing others, and not disagreeing, no matter what they think or feel about a situation. They apologize if there's a problem and may say, "I'm sorry," even if it's not their fault. If their partner gets angry, they rush in to soothe any ruffled feathers.

B. *Evading.* These partners change the topic, minimize differences, or distance themselves from any disagreement. If they sense that their partner is upset, they quickly avoid a skirmish, believing it's better to not talk about anything uncomfortable. Rather than addressing an issue head on, they may say, "Let's not spoil things by talking about that."

C. *Denying.* These individuals deny that there's a problem, even if an elephant is standing in the living room. They disconnect from their feelings and body sensations and deny any tension or discomfort. They live like the proverbial ostrich with their head in the sand. Even if they are upset in the relationship, they may say, "There's nothing wrong. I'm not upset."

Conflict Engagers

At the opposite extreme, conflict engagers do not shy away from fights. Rather, they almost look for conflict, seeing it as a contest with winners and losers. Their intention is to win arguments and put their partner on the defensive. Winning, or not losing, promotes a false sense of confidence and inflated self-esteem. Unfortunately, needing to win sets the stage for a loser, not the healthiest scenario in a relationship. If both partners adopt a pattern of conflict engaging, arguments usually spiral out of control. Some typical examples of conflict engagers include:

A. *Blaming.* These individuals attack and find fault with others. They act superior and use intimidation tactics, such a threats and aggression, to keep their partner on the defensive. They don't acknowledge their part in a problem, and focus on the flaws of the other. "You're always screwing up. You should see a therapist and get fixed!"

B. *Defending.* These partners jump to their defense at the first sign of a disagreement. They refuse to acknowledge being wrong or accept responsibility. They explain their position, as if they were in a court of law. They rationalize their behavior as perfectly normal and view their partner as the irrational one. "As I've told you countless times, there's nothing wrong with having a few drinks before I come home from work. As a matter of fact, you could probably use a drink to chill out."

C. *Complaining.* These individuals tend to be contrarians, always looking for something to complain about. They thrive on competition and view disagreements as an opportunity to joust and play the devil's advocate. If a partner says or does something positive, they'll issue a counterargument. "I don't agree." Or "That's not necessarily so."

Conflict generates anger; therefore, it's important to recognize our own style of dealing with anger and manage it differently. (Tactics to handle anger will be discussed in Chapter 11.) Our childhood programming clearly comes into play. Certain interactions with our parents and siblings trigger anger. How we responded to it in the past will be brought forward into the relationship. For example, if we felt chastised by a parent and retreated to the bedroom and sulked, we might feel the need to escape when our partner is overly critical.

While we may have learned to use one or more of the conflict evading or engaging positions, we can identify what we are doing that keeps us from receiving the love we desire, and try a different communication style. We can choose to employ mutual respect, listening, and collaboration to resolve problems. Creating an open, honest dialogue that omits criticism or blame fosters a loving environment with our partner.

Using tools such as "I" Message, open-ended questions, and active listening (mirroring what we heard) show our loved one that we respect them. Instead of informing each other of what we don't want, or demanding action, we can reframe our desires into positive requests.

Having worked with couples for the past forty years, Leonard observed that in addition to patterns, all couples experience relational cycles, just like the phases of the moon. Some individuals prefer more togetherness, while others need more separate time. Over time, the relationship establishes a norm of closeness and separateness. However, power struggles often occur where partners try to control the together and alone times.

A phase of separateness could best be described as, "I need to live my life and you need to live yours." Each of us sees ourselves as distinct individuals. From this perspective, we focus more on our differences than similarities. Polarization often occurs in this phase with one pushing for more togetherness and the other pulling away for more separateness. This phase helps us identify and explore our individual identities and emotions.

We shift into the next phase when we move away from our "self" toward "us." This can be portrayed as, "We are a team." We pay attention to the similarities and commonalities in our time together. We begin to merge desires into "us." We expand our world as we build connection and let go of our desire to satisfy only our own needs. We get joy out of fulfilling our partner's desires. The challenge is to overcome the fear of losing one's "self" or of merging too quickly.

When we gain trust that we are safe in the relationship, we move into that sweet phase, "You and I are one." There is a deepening connection into "we," giving us a feeling of connection in which we share a common vision and memorable experiences. We consciously satisfy mutual needs and nurture the relationship. This stage unites us so deeply in love that we want to shut out the rest of the world. The challenge is to maintain that blissful feeling and, at the same time, avoid total absorption into the relationship at the expense of neglecting work, other friends, and family.

The next phase moves us toward integration. This is described as, "I interact with the world as both I and we." The benefits of partnership and a joint vision are integrated into our individual lives. We hold onto the common bond while acknowledging our differences and uniqueness. We experience both connection and individuation. We can express our own needs freely within and outside of the relationship and also be attentive to and satisfy our partner's needs. The challenge is to find a balance so that we avoid moving back into "I" versus "you" or stay so enmeshed in the relationship that our individual desires get neglected.

Conflict is a signal that change is needed. It is an energy that moves couples apart and, when addressed effectively, also brings them together. If we become too entangled, conflict serves to remind us that we are unique human beings. If we become too self-absorbed, conflict alerts to reengage with our partner.

Recognizing the ebb and flow of being a unit, yet honoring our uniqueness, helps us normalize our love life. Rather than resisting the phases of union versus individualization, we can embrace the changes and use the insight to more effectively support one another as lovers.

The questions below will help you explore your repetitive responses to conflict situations. Once you gain insight into your negative patterns, you will be ready for the next chapter, which shows you how to establish respectful boundaries to create healthy relational patterns.

FIGHTING FOR LOVE EXERCISES:

1. What was your pattern of dealing with conflict as a child?

2. How do you respond to conflict as an adult in your relationship?

3. What does your partner do that triggers your frustration or anger?

4. List the situations that irritate you, e.g., your partner spends too much money on clothes, is usually late for appointments, etc.

5. What do you do that upsets your partner?

6. What could you do differently to get the response you desire?

"Yes, I remember the last time we had intimate physical contact.
We were arm wrestling for the last slice of pizza."

CHAPTER 6

Boundaries: Stay On Your Side and I'll Stay On Mine

When we fail to set boundaries and hold people accountable, we feel used and mistreated. This is why we sometimes attack who they are, which is far more hurtful than addressing a behavior or a choice.

— Brené Brown

Linda considered herself a giver. She felt true love was about never saying no to her husband, even if she didn't want to do what he asked. Trevor believed a good husband took care of his wife by controlling her. He told Linda what do, what to wear, what to say, and what friends she could have. Linda acquiesced because she enjoyed the attention, but she felt mistreated and resentful over time. Trevor would become irritated and berate her when she wouldn't oblige. Linda eventually realized it was her responsibility to establish her identity and set limits.

For many years, Linda drew her identity from her partner. She couldn't imagine who she was without the relationship. Coming from a broken home, she was willing to do anything to make her marriage work, even giving up friends and self-respect. With a lack of her own identity, she had difficulty establishing healthy boundaries. She endured emotional abuse just to save the marriage. When their youngest child graduated high school, she finally decided that she no longer could hide her true feelings.

In divorce mediation with Mari, Linda realized that she had been a volunteer in allowing Trevor to overstep her boundaries. Trevor recognized that his need to control the marriage and family made him feel like a *real* man because that was how his father ruled the household. In mediation, they each recognized their part in the relationship. To get a fair result in the dissolution, without creating an expensive courtroom battle, they agreed to define boundaries to discuss issues. Mari helped the couple speak civilly to each other. When either party failed to respect the other's boundaries, Mari stopped the escalation (she rings an Asian bell to halt conversation), and redirected them to speak in a manner that honored each other's perspectives. Since they were now living separately and respecting boundaries, they each began to communicate effectively. They figured out what they wanted and took responsibility to achieve what was most important. As a result, they created a fair agreement with the desire to attend their children's college graduations together.

Personal boundaries are the limits we set in relationships that allow us to protect ourselves emotionally as well as physically. Establishing and communicating what is or is not acceptable allows us to respect ourselves and our partner. When we have a positive sense of self-worth, we can separate our own thoughts and feelings and connect with our partner. With a conscious intention, we don't impose our way on our loved one.

Boundaries demonstrate self-awareness and acceptance. We know that we are okay and worthy as we are, yet understand that we can grow. In a healthy relationship, defined boundaries are flexible and allow us to hear what our partner wants without being rigid. At the same time, we do not give up who we are for the sake of a relationship. As we grow in a healthy, nurturing partnership, we learn mutual respect that encourages us to mature and develop as individuals.

We all have emotional and psychological needs that define how we feel safe, secure, loved, and protected. In an intimate bond, we yearn to satisfy those needs. We want to connect without losing ourselves or feeling controlled. However, in an interdependent relationship, boundary lines often are obscured. It becomes a balancing act to clarify and establish boundaries while having room for elasticity to move through life changes.

Effective communication requires us to be mindful of what we think, say, and do. Easier said than done. Intense emotions can cloud our thinking. In times of stress, we may either overstep our own boundaries or allow them to be trampled.

As we grew up, we tested out what we could get away with parents, teachers, friends, and partners. We developed emotional intelligence through trial and error as we figured out what was reasonable for us and for others. We found out what we could live with and what made us comfortable. We then consciously and unconsciously used those experiences to establish boundaries with others. In chapter 2, we discussed how childhood experiences taught us how to deal with anger and conflict. Our upbringing modeled ways to create boundaries and either respect or over-step them. Ask yourself these questions:

1. How well did your parents institute boundaries with each other and with you when you lived at home?

2. How balanced was your parents' relationship? Did your mother or your father control the relationship?

3. Who overstepped boundaries? How did the other parent react?

4. What boundaries did you experience growing up? Did you have the privacy of your own room? Were there reasonable restrictions?

5. How do you engage in conflict by repeating either of your parents' behaviors?

The following situations often generate conflict. How do you relate to the statements below? Do you believe they are true or false for you or your loved one?

T or F: When my partner doesn't want to go where I wish to go or do what I want to do, I get angry or withdraw emotionally.

T or F: When my loved one confronts me on an issue, I blame him/her.

T or F: If my lover disagrees with me, we have an argument.

T or F: My mood depends on how my partner behaves.

T or F: If I am upset about something, I suppress my feelings and pretend that everything is all right.

T or F: I have to lie to my loved one so I don't have to experience his/her wrath.

T or F: I nag my partner to do something that I want.

T or F: Instead of talking directly to my partner, I tell my friends about our problems.

After considering the above statements, answer the questions below:

1. Did your parents demonstrate any of these behaviors?

2. How did these actions create conflict?

3. How does each of these behaviors affect your ability to create healthy boundaries?

4. If you answered true to any of the above behaviors, how might you act differently in the future?

We often unconsciously treat boundaries just as we experienced them in childhood and in previous relationships. With recognition of our negative reactions, we can reduce conflict by speaking up and telling how we feel. When we express what is uncomfortable without blame, we take a step toward establishing acceptable boundaries. Honestly sharing what makes us feel hurt, disrespected, or devalued creates a climate for increased understanding and intimacy. As we assess and clarify what feels good and what feel terrible, we define boundaries with each other.

Self-awareness helps us become aware of and communicate our needs and desires. When we are clear about what we really need, we show love and acceptance of ourselves and are better able to appreciate and love those qualities that make our lover unique.

Long-time married couples often tell us that the secret to their marriage longevity is that they allow each other to be who they really are. They communicate what they want in a respectful way. Each partner takes responsibility to notify the other in a kind manner of what is or is not comfortable. They negotiate healthy boundaries that create the freedom to be who they are as individuals and interdependent love partners.

Sarah and Phillip sought counseling because their sex lives had become dissatisfying. They both were raised Catholic and had considerable guilt about intimate pleasure. Neither felt comfortable talking about what they really enjoyed. They expected the other to intuitively know what to do. Sarah preferred more assertive lovemaking but was embarrassed to make requests. Phillip, on the other hand, felt controlled and became less responsive when Sarah took the lead. In counseling, Leonard helped the couple open a dialogue about their sexual needs. They explored ways to create more pleasure while respecting the other person's wishes. As each became more comfortable expressing their desires and making requests, they released their guilt and opened up their sex lives. Passion and pleasure became a regular part of their relationship.

When Mari works with couples in mediation, one partner may say what he or she thinks is best for the children. In response, the other parent may blow up in a rage, instead of explaining concerns and making a counterproposal. That behavior exemplifies an inability to mutually respect boundaries. Mari shows couples how to ask for what they want, not what they don't want, so they can de-escalate conflict and engage in creating solutions.

Generally, when a boundary is crossed, hostility erupts. Setting limits may create tension, if not done tactfully. In order to establish healthy boundaries, consider the following steps:

1. Explore and analyze what is acceptable and unacceptable for yourself first. Then consider how that affects the relationship. For example, if you are in a committed relationship and expect your partner to be monogamous, you might state, "It's important for me to be in a monogamous relationship. I would feel unsafe if you had sex outside the relationship." That statement sets a boundary and if the issue cannot be respected, you cannot continue to be together.

2. Clarify your beliefs about emotional and physical intimacy. You and your loved one can clarify the limits of affection. For example, if you believe any display of affection in public is unacceptable because you learned that as a child, you may want to reassess how that belief affects your present relationship.

Many couples like to text to stay connected. However, it's important not to overstep boundaries. For example, Julie likes to text Jared love messages many times during the day. When Jared is at work, he's unable to respond until he is on a break. This irritates Julie who wants an immediate response. When she doesn't get an answer, she starts flooding him with messages, "Why aren't you answering me? What are you doing?" By the time Jared arrives home, he's furious.

If this couple clarified their texting relationship, they could establish an agreement about the best times and places to send and receive messages.

3. Identify whether you say yes to your partner when you really want to say no. Do you say "yes" to make the other person happy? Can you say "no" in a positive way without feeling guilty? There is power in saying a positive no, such as, "I would love to help you, but this is not a good time. I can do that for you later this afternoon." When setting your limits, consider if and when you can accommodate.

4. Question whether your boundaries are congruent with your current values. You automatically repeat learned values from your parents without questioning them. Evaluate whether those values still apply to your life now. For example, "I avoid kissing my spouse in front of the children because my parents never showed affection in front of the kids." You may reconsider that showing affection models to your children that you and your spouse love each other.

5. Take responsibility for your choices, thoughts, behaviors, and words without blaming your partner. You are the one in control of your life. If you blame someone else, you become the victim. You empower yourself when you make decisions about your own actions. For example, instead of expressing, "My wife won't let me drink booze anymore," you can say, "I choose to not to drink alcohol for my health."

6. Release being responsible for your lover's thoughts, actions, and words. You are only in charge of yourself, and that is hard enough to manage. You show your love when you mutually support one another. For example, if your partner asks you what he or she should do about taking a new job, you could answer, "What do you think is best for you? What are the advantages and disadvantages?"

7. Respond in a neutral tone when your significant other says something hurtful or upsetting. Be direct and set limits in your response, using "I" Messages such as, "I feel hurt and upset when I am called derogatory names. I'm not comfortable with an attack and don't want to engage." It may not be easy to respond like this when you feel attacked by your loved one, but recognizing that you have the power to set your limits helps you focus on what you can do, instead of reacting with your own hurtful statement.

8. Respect your partner's choice, honor their decision, and be open to negotiation. For example, your partner says, "I don't feel up to going to your parents' home today." You can ask why and then acknowledge their decision with "I understand." Sometimes, there is room for negotiation. Without nagging, you might say, "If you spend two hours with me at my parents' home, then afterwards we can go to the movie you wanted to see." If your partner says he is too tired, then your respectful acceptance of his feelings shows loving consideration. Once boundaries are clarified after a calm and fair negotiation, accept and appreciate the final decision.

Another way of respecting your partner's choice is to ask on a scale of one to ten, with ten being a resounding yes and one a clear no, how she or he feels about doing something. For example, if you want to go to a movie and you assign your desire as an eight, yet your partner only gives it a two, you may decide on an alternative movie where you both rank it as a five or above.

9. Talk to each other without blaming, accusing, demeaning, or disparaging. No matter how angry you are, stop yourself from reacting or saying harmful words until you calm down. Separate the person from the problem and focus on behavior, not character. Instead of saying, "You're wrong," you can say, "I see it differently."

10. When you feel your boundaries are crossed, keep calm, and gently and assertively let your partner know of your discomfort. Be consistent. Use the words, "I'm not comfortable with…" For example, if your loved one refuses to allow your own children from a previous marriage to visit, you can let him or her know that you want to see your children in your home. If there are behavior problems with the children, you can set appropriate boundaries with them.

The bottom line is that setting boundaries is not about controlling anyone but yourself. It is about acknowledging what is acceptable for you and learning your own self-control. The greatest growth in your relationship will occur when you accept that only you are responsible for how you manage your own emotions and how you respond to your partner's behavior.

The following statements below will help you determine if you are taking responsibility for your own life or are focused on the boundaries of your lover. Share your responses with your partner and discuss the issues.

Rate each statement as: **A for Always, S for Sometimes, or N for Never.**

A S N: I can be myself when I am with my loved one.

A S N: I can ask for what I want without fearing rejection.

A S N: I know that I am responsible for my own happiness.

A S N: I refrain from blaming or accusing my loved one.

A S N: I am receptive to constructive feedback from my partner.

A S N: I gain understanding when we have an honest discussion.

A S N: I do not become defensive when I hear suggestions.

A S N: I ask for clarification when I am confused about my loved one's thoughts.

A S N: I accept responsibility for my attitudes, choices, and behaviors.

A S N: I am able to forgive my partner and move forward.

A S N: I am capable of managing my anger.

A S N: I am trusting, open, and honest.

A S N: I am willing to admit mistakes.

A S N: I give honest feedback to my lover without being offensive.

A S N: I respect my loved one's boundaries.

Share your answers with your partner and discuss how the two of you can respond more positively.

When you communicate limits to each other, jointly establish agreed-upon consequences if your boundaries are violated. Without ramifications, there is no motivation to change behaviors. We all learn by cause and effect.

Therefore, it is better if you and your partner develop consequences together. If that is not possible, create a fair consequence that is reasonable. Let your lover know ahead of time what will happen and give him/her a fair warning. That way your partner will have a choice to respect your requests.

Consequences are best when they are fair and pre-warned responses to disrespectful boundary violations. Setting appropriate limits are not attempts to control each other. And when you do respond, act in a calm and deliberate manner, not with an angry threat. Here are a few examples to say in a calm tone of voice:

"If you have another beer before we go to the party, I will stay home."

"If you continue to scream at me, I will leave the room."

"If you spend more money for nonessentials this month, we can't go out to dinner next weekend."

Consequences have to be appropriate, and not out of proportion, to the behavior you wish to stop. If you partner yells at you on the phone, let her or him know that if she/he continues to yell, you will gently hang up. However, it wouldn't be appropriate to move out or threaten divorce. If you threaten something severe in anger and do not follow through, the proposed consequence has no meaning. It only causes further disconnection. Your partner won't respect your warnings, and you won't feel good about yourself. Before you consider a warning, get centered and think through the consequence as fitting to the circumstance.

When boundaries are violated, calmly state the appropriate warning. Be willing to follow through, unless the situation changes. If your loved one changes his/her attitude or behavior, drop the consequences.

Just as we establish immediate, specific, and consistent consequences with children and pets, we can do this with our lovers. If the offensive behavior ceases, then reward your sweetheart with gratitude and affection.

Warning: Avoid using consequences as retaliation. Saying, "If you don't go with me to visit my family, I won't have sex with you for two weeks," would create a hostile response. Withholding love and lovemaking in this instance is more of a reprisal and does not relate to a visit with family members. All consequences should show respect for each other and the relationship and not be punitive.

If you have to impose consequences for your partner's failure to respect your boundary, follow through in a neutral tone of voice and don't hold a grudge. Afterward, be willing to forgive. That does not mean that you condone the behavior. Instead, forgiveness sets you free from painful resentment and opens your heart to reconnect.

After the situation has resolved, discuss the issues without laying a guilt trip. If you attack your partner for overstepping your boundaries, your blaming approach, in essence, violates your partner's boundaries. Every time you act calmly with dignity and compassion, you increase your partner's respect for you.

Negotiating and honoring reasonable limits teaches you and your partner to value each other's uniqueness. If you can love not only the agreeable aspects of each other, but also appreciate your unique individual limits, you will boost each other's self-esteem. You may not always get everything you want, but you will know what is acceptable ahead of time and find other ways to get your needs met. For example, if your partner hates horror movies, you can jointly attend movies that you both enjoy. But you can also see the scary movies with other friends.

Just as good fences make good neighbors, good boundaries make good lovers. You can be close and intimate and still let the wind blow between you. Clear limits enable you to voluntarily curb behaviors that offend your partner and expand behaviors that demonstrate love. Healthy, considerate boundaries create strong bonds that foster intimacy. You can then build passionate bridges of connection, the subject of the next chapter.

FIGHTING FOR LOVE EXERCISES:

Consider a situation where you felt your boundaries were invaded by your partner, such as getting interrupted on the phone, opening your mail, finishing your sentences, reading your email, nagging, etc.

1. How did you and your partner deal with the conflict?

2. What might you do differently?

3. When you feel your boundaries are crossed, how can you effectively communicate what you want to your partner?

4. Make a list of how you may be crossing your partner's boundaries and consider how you could modify your words and actions to show respect.

5. What boundaries or limits do you want in your relationship?

6. How might you be flexible with your boundaries to accommodate your loved one yet still be respectful of your comfort zone?

Boundaries are, in simple terms, the recognition of personal space.

— Asa Don Brown

"You and I make a great team. But I wish we'd score more often!"

CHAPTER 7

Build Bridges—the Love Connection

We build too many walls and not enough bridges.

— Isaac Newton

Roxanne and Stewart constantly argued about finances. Roxanne complained that Stewart spent money foolishly on gadgets. He argued back that he had a right to spend the money he earned. Each fought for their position, but, in the process, neither one felt heard or understood. Roxanne often pointed her finger accusingly at Stewart. He responded by crossing his arms.

This scenario clearly represented a win/lose proposition. Roxanne and Stewart had adopted defensive postures and erected walls that became fixed rigid positions. No amount of arguing would penetrate each other's defenses. Their brains, alerting them to protect themselves from attack, produced chemicals to help them fight or flee. Their senses scanned for further signs of threat as their bodies prepared for battle. Stewart's shoulders rose to his neck. Roxanne's hand clenched into a fist. Both faces flushed with anger, their breathing quickened, and heart rates rose.

Clearly, this couple didn't need to erect any more defenses, unless they wanted to continue the battle. If they could observe themselves, they would have recognized the anger displayed in their bodies, emotional reactions, and voice tones. They would have felt the physical tension and the growing disconnection. They could have used the heightened awareness to pause and ask themselves these questions:

- What am I feeling?

- What are we really arguing about?

- What do I need or desire from my partner?

- What does my partner need or desire from me?

- What could I do to break the impasse and respond in a loving manner?

These questions start a shift in thinking, from defensiveness and rigidity toward openness, problem solving, and the dissolving of defenses. Answering these questions helps us lower the drawbridge and see a path for loving, intimate connection.

When we become defensive, we automatically erect rigid walls to protect ourselves. While boundaries serve to protect and establish identities, to honor the "I," defensiveness and rigid boundaries prevent us from coming together as "we." If we are only concerned about what we want, at the expense of our mate, that leads to conflict.

Conflict is the gift that reminds us that we have something to learn. We can choose either to maintain dividing walls or to establish bridges of connection. Healthy couples balance individuality and connection. They create comfortable boundaries and build bridges of understanding to connect. Some individuals are proficient at being self-sufficient and independent, while others are better at being dependent and connected. Traditionally, men value rugged individualism, while women embrace connection in relationships. However, those stereotypes are changing. All of us can respectfully negotiate when to unite and when to allow for separateness.

To establish greater intimacy, we must first recognize when we raised the drawbridge to keep our partner out. Our senses and emotions alert us when we or our partner have erected barricades. On the positive side, emotional defenses protect our psyche and maintain our identity. They help us take control of life and make judgments about what we perceive to be right or wrong. Self-control and judgments enable us to survive in a world where decisions have to be made quickly, especially when we are threatened. In a love relationship, we need to become aware of the times when we shift into survival mode, build roadblocks, and make assumptions about our partner through judgments that may or may not be accurate.

Jennifer and Tony had been dating for two years. Tony often spends a great deal of time on social media sites and gets easily distracted by his iPhone. Tony is a social butterfly while Jennifer is more reserved. She often checks up on his social networking pages. One day, she noticed that Tony had "liked" another girl's post on social media. This made Jennifer very insecure about their relationship. Over dinner, Jennifer opened up the conversation.

Jennifer: *So, how's Monica?*

Tony: *Huh? She's fine, I guess? Why do you ask?*

Jennifer: *Oh, nothing.*

Tony: *Okay.*

After dinner, Jennifer notices Tony smiling while staring at his phone.

Jennifer: *So, when was the last time you and Monica talked?*

Tony: *Ugh… A few months ago, I guess? Why are you asking me stupid questions?*

Jennifer: *Because you seem pretty interested in her!*

Tony: *What the hell are you talking about?*

Jennifer: *You're obviously busy on her page, liking her posts, and clearly talking to her. Why else are you smiling and looking at your phone?*

Tony: *Whoa. You're totally wrong.*

Jennifer: *Well, you're ignoring me for her. Why don't you just go talk to her!*

Tony: *I'm just playing games. Look!*

Tony shows her his phone.

Jennifer: *Whatever, I don't care.*

Jennifer's insecurities caused her to assume the worse in an innocent situation. Tony's inability to communicate and notice Jennifer's needs added fuel to Jennifer's suspicions.

Fear often makes us feel threatened and pushes us to try to control a situation by blaming, accusing, or criticizing our partner. Anger, frustration, and misunderstandings cause us to raise our personal drawbridge and retreat behind the protected castle of our ego. If we hide behind walls and sling arrows over the ramparts, the result is war.

Conscious awareness of our reaction to an upset helps us recognize when we have retreated and erected defenses to protect ourselves. Conflict offers us a gift, an alarm, a choice to look within at how we feel, so we can then rebuild a bridge of connection. When we become calm and avoid blaming or judging, we can approach our loved one in dialogue with an open heart. If we want to hear what our partner says, we must open the door, remain open and present, and drop the need to be defensive. Ultimately, bridge building begins with deeply listening to our partner.

Tony could pause, conscious of Jennifer's fears, open his heart to her, and reassure her that she is the only one for him. Then he could ask her what she needs to feel safe in the relationship. By opening the dialogue, about what is acceptable and uncomfortable when using social media, they can come to some agreement.

When couples first enter therapy, they often point the finger at each other.

"Stewart needs to change his spending habits," complains Roxanne.

He huffs, "My wife has to quit complaining. All I hear is nothing but complaints."

She retaliates, "If you will manage money more responsibly, I won't complain."

Couples in conflict hurtle rocks from their respective fortresses. They can choose to stop throwing them and wave a white flag of truce. When they stop the accusations and focus on expressing their underlying concerns and feelings, they could then negotiate terms of agreement, as discussed in Chapter 10.

Let's look at how the following accusations build a wall between Beth and Jordan.

The blame game: erecting a wall

Beth: *You never help me get ready for a dinner party with your family.*

Jordan: *You planned it and then told me about it, so deal with it. You always set up parties without asking me whether I want them.*

Needless to say, Beth had to set up, cook the meal, and clean the house. Neither partner was happy when the family arrived.

Building a bridge

The couple could stop the accusations and build a bridge of understanding by expressing their needs:

Beth: *Honey, your mom asked if your family can visit tomorrow. How do you feel about making a BBQ, and I clean up and make veggies?*

Jordan: *Babe, I was hoping to just rest tomorrow. I wanted to sleep in and relax on Saturday.*

Beth: *What should I tell your mom?*

Jordan: *Ask her if she wants to come on Sunday instead, for an early dinner. I'll cook salmon outside on the BBQ. Could you clean up and set up for dinner?*

Beth: *It's a deal.*

In the above scenario, both respected and honored each other's feelings, and created a bridge of connection. Notice that they also acknowledged boundaries of comfort and discomfort.

Unfortunately, this type of negotiation doesn't happen without a conscious effort. When lovers feel attacked, they take the position, "If you change, then I'll change, but you have to change first. If you don't change, I won't change." This conveys a win-lose attitude of wanting to remain in control. If someone wants to prove she or he is right, the argument will escalate, leading to another retreat and more rock throwing.

How can we build a strong connection and find ways of understanding our differences so that fortresses and weapons become unnecessary? With conscious effort, we can release the need to blame, criticize, and control the relationship, as well as the outcome, and respectfully address each other's concerns. As the drawbridge lowers, we step forward onto the bridge of connection.

To stop the blame and control game, we need to refrain from overtly or covertly manipulating our partner to change. If we criticize certain behaviors, obviously that is an overt attempt at control. If we sulk or use fear or sex to get our way, we covertly try to control the relationship. Usually, when we feel blamed, accused, or controlled, we want to escape. That sends a message of rejection to our partner. Instead, we can release the need to win or be right, take some deep breaths, and be receptive to hearing our loved one without defensiveness. That breaks the battle cycle.

If we view our partner as the enemy, we close the door to connection. As Albert Einstein once wrote, "A human being...experiences himself, his thoughts and feelings as something separated from the rest—a kind of optical delusion of his consciousness. This delusion is a kind of prison for us. ... Our task must be to free ourselves from this prison by widening our circles of compassion to embrace all living creatures and the whole of nature in its beauty."

To break free from the prison of loneliness, we start by:

1. Recognizing how we feel.

2. Examining what causes us to feel separate.

3. Expressing our perceptions and feelings to our partner.

4. Consciously letting go of our need to dictate the behavior of our partner.

5. Finding out how our partner sees the situation.

6. Acknowledging our commonalities.

7. Thanking our partner for being open to express thoughts and feelings.

Each of us holds the key to unlock the prison door that separates us from one another. As we surrender to what is happening in the now, in compassionate communication, we open the gates to meet each other. Eckhart Tolle's book, *The Power of Now*, presents the concept that the power of living resides in the present moment. Doing so means surrendering thoughts about past problems or worrying about future challenges. It's about being mindful minute by minute.

We cannot change what has happened to us even one minute ago. Staying aware of the present moment forces us to give up focusing on past regrets or fears of the future. It encourages us to be an observer of our feelings and sensations and to those of our partner right now. It allows us to open up a dialogue about what is currently happening so we don't blame or induce guilt.

Instead of Roxanne blaming her spouse, "You never act responsibly about money," she could say, "I'm feeling scared about not having enough money. It makes me sick to my stomach." That would open up a different conversation with Stewart. He could reply, "When it comes to money, I get defensive and tense and don't feel comfortable talking about it."

Once they refrain from blaming, they can refocus on understanding one another. As they eliminate judging, each can explore perspectives without attacking or creating defensive walls.

Ever since we were children, we yearned for unconditional love without judgment. Most of us do not feel unconditional love from our partner, for the ego continually looks for ways to be right. We each have our own perception of the truth, depending on how we view the world. Often we each see situations differently. When we stop defending against attacks, we observe the world more innocently, like children.

Healthy, young children overflow with imagination, wonder, spontaneity, trust, and love. They delight in their bodies, display their emotions easily, have inquisitive minds, and live in the moment. They express themselves freely and giggle, laugh, and play with abandon.

A young child lives in the now and recognizes beauty in the world. She or he may stare wide-eyed at the twinkling stars, color a picture with single-minded intensity, snuggle into a parent's arms, delight in blowing bubbles, and have an unwavering curiosity about the world. And when a child gets angry, he or she quickly gets over it.

The Chinese sage Quan Yin reminds us, "As children do not judge, nor do they intend harm, loving kindness is always easiest to express to them. Learning from this experience, one can begin to treat each other as if he was a child."

When we look upon our partner as an innocent child, knowing that she/he can be easily wounded and hurt, we are better able to set aside our need to be right and embrace our lover with wonder and love. We are more apt to discover something new about them. We can leave the confines of our separateness, as if in an isolated castle, and enter a sacred space to be playful and receptive to connect deeply. Acting from the place of childhood innocence promotes a joyful interaction where we can leave our fortress and establish a bridge to our partner's heart.

Mirror your partner

Research shows that when we connect with someone, our brain fires mirror neurons that reflect the emotional state of another person. When partners feel in sync, we begin to adopt similar body postures, breathe rhythmically, and use a tone of voice that soothes and connects us to one another.

By mirroring our partner, we create a bridge of connection. Mirroring happens automatically when we feel loved; however, if there is a falling out and walls have appeared, we can deliberately shift the energy. We can move physically closer, hold hands, hug, or gaze lovingly into each other's eyes. Breath is a great connector. We can consciously breathe in rhythm with our partner or take deep slow breaths to relax our partner.

Harville Hendrix in his book, *Getting the Love You Want*, describes a dialogue process that involves three parts—mirroring, validation, and empathy.[6] Mirroring

---

6   Hendrix, Harville, *Getting the Love You Want: A Guide for Couples*, New York: St. Martin's Press, 2007; pp. 142-153.

is a form of active listening, where you reflect back what your partner says. For example, "What I hear you saying is…" After your partner finishes what he/she wants to say, you continue to ask your partner to clarify by asking, "Is there more?"

Once your partner feels heard, you validate him or her by acknowledging and summarizing and letting it be known that what was said made sense. And when you have really heard your partner, you move to a deeper understanding of her or his thoughts and feelings. As a loving wrap-up, you can validate that your partner worked through a difficult conflict with you.

Empathy occurs naturally in your partner when you express how you feel in a non-offensive manner. A heartfelt connection occurs when you experience what your partner is going through. If you feel each other's pain and the longing for connection, and convey that sensitivity to your lover, you move closer to each another.

DISCOVER YOUR LANGUAGE OF LOVE

Sitting in Leonard's office, Emma scowled at Victor. She then turned to Leonard and said, "I tell my husband all the time that I love him. He rarely says those words to me. Sure, he takes me out to dinner, washes my car, and buys me flowers, but I wish he'd let me know that he loved me!" What Emma didn't realize was that Victor, in his own way, had been expressing love differently than his wife.

Gary Chapman, a therapist and the author of *The 5 Love Languages: The Secret to Love that Lasts*, identified five languages of love that convey the emotion that we are loved.[7] We may:

1. Speak words to express appreciation and love.

2. Use touch to communicate affection.

3. Provide quality time to convey specialness.

4. Commit acts of service to suggest caring.

5. Give gifts to deliver the message that our partner is important.

Though each of us tends to use the language of love that we prefer for ourselves, this doesn't always communicate love to our partner. Our loved one may resonate with another love language. Communicating to our partner in a way that makes him or her feel loved generates more love.

In the above scenario, Emma yearned to hear loving words, whereas Victor expressed love through acts of service and gifts. They clearly missed the mark every time they expressed love. Emma complained that Victor wasn't romantic because he didn't verbally express his love, while her husband grumbled that Emma was never satisfied with all that he did for her. Each simmered behind walls of resentment. In counseling, they learned to communicate love in their partner's language. Victor began to tell Emma verbally how much he loved her,

---

7   Chapman, Gary, *The 5 Love Languages: The Secret to Love that Last*, Chicago: Northfield Publishing, 2010; pp. 123-131.

and she spent more time helping Victor and bringing him gifts. As a result, they both experienced more love in their relationship.

Words of Appreciation

The first love language consists of words of praise, appreciation, and love. The words, "I love you, care about you, and cherish you," have an enormous impact on those who need words of affection and praise. If someone rarely heard verbal recognition as a child, they would probably want their partner to express love and caring through affirming words.

One exercise to satisfy this language of love is for both partners to start and end the day with appreciations. For example, "I appreciate you being in my life and love being with you."

Touch and Affection

Some individuals prefer the second language of love, namely, touch and affection. For them, holding hands and hugging create a physical and emotional connection that reduces barriers and creates intimacy. These partners prefer sensory touch, including massage and lovemaking, to bond the relationship and may view the absence of it as indifference, neglect, or abandonment.

A great exercise to minimize tension and increase intimacy is to hold your partner and take a deep breath. This signals your loved one to do the same. You might even lie down together into a spooning position and mirror your partner's breathing. This is more effective without talking. When your energy is centered, you shift the physiology. After a while, you both will relax and merge into one another.

Quality Time

The third way to express love is through quality time. Partners who resonate with this language feel important and special when their lover makes time to be with them. Listening to music together, shared meals, conversation, even shopping as a couple, are ways that convey love to these individuals.

You could take turns organizing a romantic getaway from work and the children. Having a date on the calendar insures quality time to reconnect.

Acts of Service

Some partners prefer acts of service, the fourth love language. Men have traditionally shown their love through doing and fixing, while women often prepared meals as a sign of nurturing. Individuals who respond to acts of service, such as arranging babysitters, helping out with projects, or taking care of chores, feel valued, especially when their requests are met.

To encourage acts of service, make a list of activities that promote the feeling of love. Then randomly choose some of them to create more love in your relationship, like foot rubs, massage, wash the car, make dinner, do the laundry, etc.

Giving Gifts

Giving and receiving gifts is the last language of love. Flowers, chocolate, cards, love letters, or surprises generate feelings of love and appreciation. These partners need to receive the message, through gifts, that they are remembered and special. The way to the heart is through a thoughtful present.

Check with your partner about the type of gifts that he or she prefers. A man may enjoy a set of golf balls while a woman may relish a certificate to get her nails done. More importantly, it's the thought about giving a gift that counts.

As you recognize your own love language, you might also ask which language of love helps your partner feel cherished. You may be showing your partner what you would prefer them to do for you. If you enjoy affection and touch and act in that manner with a lover who prefers quality time and acts of service, you both may feel dissatisfied. So use the language of love that makes your partner feel desired.

Positive Statements to Each Other

Positive words and actions reinforce a loving bond. The renowned expert on couples, Dr. John Gottman, identified in his research that one of the main determinants in couple satisfaction or dissatisfaction was the ratio of positives to negatives in their interactions. To have a positive, growing relationship, the ratio should be five positive statements or actions to one negative. A positive climate reinforced with affirming acts and loving words creates a zone of safety, caring, and security. In such an environment, concerns and differences of opinion do not threaten the relationship and issues can be easily resolved.

If you acknowledge to each other the importance of your relationship on a regular basis, in a variety of love languages, you reinforce bridge building. Your random acts of love every day keep your walls down and your love quota high.

Sexual connection and intimacy

We can't end this chapter on building bridges of connection without talking about the importance of sex and intimacy. A love relationship usually needs sexual connection to glue the couple together. Sex without intimacy can feel empty, while intimacy without sex can generate frustration. Combine sex with intimacy, and you have a potent force to release stress, create connection, and strengthen bonds. Lovemaking incorporates the five love languages of touch, words, quality time, acts of service, and gifts.

Sex can be a beautiful way for you and your partner to play together and add fun and pleasure to your lives. Sexual pleasure generates positive brain chemicals such as testosterone, dopamine, oxytocin, and serotonin to generate passion and a lustful desire for union. If you and your lover enjoy bedroom pleasure, you may wonder why you don't do it more often. Some of the reasons may be: stress; resentment; lack of communication; disconnection; different sex drives; exhaustion; or health issues.

Men and women seem to have different expectations and needs. Men often need sex to feel close and women need to feel connected to enjoy sex. If you or your partner need emotional intimacy before making love, or your partner needs a physical release to feel close, discuss the differences and find ways to meet each other's needs. When emotional needs are not met, sex can easily turn into a battleground instead of a play-ground. However, if you and your partner communicate and resolve misunderstandings, making up will lead to a night (or morning) of ecstasy.

So how can couples use sex to play together and expand love and intimacy? Consider Christopher and Peggy, who were married fifteen years. After watching their sex lives diminish after the birth of their children, they decided to create more passion in their relationship. They arranged to have their grammar-school children looked after by one set of grandparents each Friday evening as their date night. Fortunately, both grandparents and children were eager to spend time together.

Christopher and Peggy took turns dropping off the children. The other partner would prepare the evening of passion and set up the playground. One might serve a lovely meal with their favorite wine before adjourning to the bedroom for dessert. The other might set up the massage table for an evening of sensuous touch. The couple treated the evening as a time to take a break from their hectic schedules and play together.

Each Friday offered them an opportunity to strengthen their bond. Sometimes, they would read books or watch videos on Tantric sex (based on Eastern sexual practices that incorporate ritual to heighten consciousness). Other times, they would act out fantasies, or just cuddle up to each other on the couch. They gave each other feedback about what felt pleasurable and took turns giving and receiving. If Christopher was tired after a difficult week, he would request a massage to ease the tension. When Peggy needed time to talk about the week, Christopher would listen. In this way, each had their needs satisfied by making requests and having them met. This date night replenished them, particularly when they both were stressed. When it came to the end of the week, they would breathe a sigh of relief and exclaim, "Thank God, it's Friday!" The benefits of the connection from the date night spilled over into the rest of the week so that they could feel close, even when at work.

Now you may not be as inventive or playful as Christopher and Peggy, but you can create more intimacy and sexual pleasure by watching romantic movies, attending love-enhancing seminars, reading books together on relationships, giving each other massages, and playing together in sports or other physical activity.

Sexual intimacy is about expanding awareness and connection; therefore, the goal is not to rush toward orgasm. Rather, it's about creating a loving space to be present to our partner's sexual and emotional needs, as well as our own. When we release thoughts of the day and focus on our senses — smell, taste, touch, sounds, and sight — we can enjoy the moment without worrying about performance. Keep in mind that the goal is not to cross the finish line but to savor the journey of giving and receiving pleasure.

Bedrooms typically become the arena for lovemaking; however, romantic scenes can take place in the living room, bathtub, or in the kitchen. Consider how you can best set the mood and intention for a night of lovemaking, then create a romantic playground with candles, incense, music, lingerie, and silk underwear. Experiment with variety to add some spice.

For those who have grown up with sexual inhibitions and beliefs that sex was evil or dirty, set aside some time to share your feelings with your partner away from the bedroom. Be patient with one another as you discuss what holds you back from giving or receiving pleasure. An honest discussion opens the door for genuine intimacy where you can feel vulnerable and safe.

The bonding tools outlined in this chapter will help you and your partner build bridges of connection. If you have difficulty opening your heart, you may need to focus on the practice of forgiveness, the topic of the next chapter.

FIGHTING FOR LOVE EXERCISES:

1. Think of a time when you felt defensive and put up a wall in the relationship.

   a. How did you experience the tension, and what did you think and do?
   b. What could you have done to build a bridge of connection?

2. What is your language of love?

3. What is your partner's language of love?

4. What can you do to express love to your partner in his or her language?

5. Name some ways that you can turn up the heat in your relationship.

6. Describe your ideal Date Night.

7. How can you enhance your lovemaking?

"I'm trying to develop an 'attitude of gratitude' but
the best I can muster is a 'sentiment of resentment'."

CHAPTER 8

Forgive Me Not; Forgive Me

*The weak can never forgive. Forgiveness
is the attribute of the strong.*

— Mahatma Gandhi

When Amy learned that her husband had gambled and lost $5000 at the casino, she became furious. That money was planned for a much-needed vacation to celebrate their upcoming anniversary. Jack had never gambled huge sums, but he naively hoped to win big at a casino and take Amy on a luxurious cruise. He begged her forgiveness and promised to work overtime, never gamble again, and replenish the lost funds. While Amy loved Jack, she couldn't let go of her anger. Jack didn't think he could forgive himself either.

One of the most difficult challenges in fighting for love is the practice of forgiveness. When we feel betrayed or hurt by our intimate partner, it may seem like our heart is broken or torn from our chest. We may feel victimized, disrespected, or unloved. The deep hurt can turn to anger and cause us to seek revenge. Our natural tendency is to defend ourselves, blame, or criticize our partner and repeat stories of how were betrayed or victimized. When our partner deceives us or lets us down, sense of self may feel threatened.

Our ego often has an investment in self-righteousness about our feelings. We want to make sure our partner knows what they have done that was so wrong. However, an attitude of blame merely locks us into a power struggle about who is right or wrong. Even if our partner hurt us badly by something she or he said or did, we need to forgive and let go. Forgiveness frees us from living in agony. It's our salvation from reliving over and over the hell of what was said or done. Forgiving does not mean forgetting. Instead, it is a letting go of the repetitive memories of pain. Holding on to the past debilitates us and keeps us from truly connecting again. We forgive our loved one as a gift for ourselves so we are not shackled to the negativity from a past that cannot be changed. Forgiveness releases us from the prison of hurtful emotions.

Nelson Mandela spent twenty-seven years of his life in prison. He had every reason not to forgive his jailers when he was released. Yet when asked by President Clinton if he hated those who put him in prison, he answered, "I felt hatred and fear, but I said to myself, if you hate them when you get into that car, you will still be their prisoner. I wanted to be free and so I let go."

Nelson Mandela inspired thousands of others to forgive, as he once said, "Resentment is like drinking poison and then hoping it will kill your enemies." Holding onto the bitterness creates physical and psychological problems, whereas, forgiveness helps us let go of the toxins that destroy relationships. Suppressed emotional wounds linger in our subconscious, even after we have forgotten the details of what happened. When we hold on to the upsetting past stories, they remain emotionally charged. Healing requires that we clear out the distressing memories, just as we would clean a physical wound of irritating debris. If we neglect the wound, it will aggravate us until we become ill and act to heal our body. Emotional slivers of resentment are signals to attend to the wound and let go.

Before we share the steps of how to forgive, let's clear up some misconceptions. Forgiveness does *not* mean that we tolerate or condone someone's wrongdoing, nor does it mean that we forget the incidents that caused us pain. Remembering them reminds us to change our thinking, create appropriate boundaries, and not allow ourselves to be treated in a way that causes us to resent ourselves and our loved ones.

In the case above, where Jack lost $5,000 gambling, Jill has a choice to stew in the anger for what happened, (which would probably create more animosity and make her sick) or move beyond the anger and use the experience to clarify what she needs going forward. This couple could learn from the painful experience and address the issue of Jack's gambling and how money will be spent by each of them in the future so the situation wouldn't happen again.

The book *A Course in Miracles* points out that the unforgiving mind is full of fear and despair, seeing little hope for reconciliation. The forgiving mind releases negative feelings about a past situation and accepts that the past is over. The ultimate goal is to replace the past hurtful thoughts with positive or neutral thoughts. Forgiveness is a process of consciously shifting our thinking away from disturbing images, thoughts, memories, and feelings that chain us from moving forward joyfully. Letting go provides relief from inner turmoil and offers peace and serenity.

Just as it is important to forgive others, it is critical to forgive ourselves for any hurt or pain we may have caused our loved ones. Instead of mentally beating ourselves up with thoughts such as, "It's my fault that my spouse found someone else," or "I should know better than to say things like that to my wife," we could say, "I forgive myself for what happened, and I will be more mindful not to attack when I get angry." Or if we tell ourselves, "I'm always making mistakes," we can say, "I forgive myself for this error and I will learn from it."

Maya Angelou reinforced the message of self-forgiveness: "If you live, you will make mistakes. It is inevitable. But once you do and you see the mistake, then you forgive yourself... If we all hold on to the mistake, we can't see our own glory in the mirror because we have the mistake between our faces and the mirror."

Since our childhood programming operates in the background, we unconsciously replicate similar relationships from the past in order to resolve those issues and get our needs met in the present. Becoming aware of those patterns allows us to give up old resentments and move forward with a clean slate.

Forgiveness sets us free from the bondage and agony of old messages and harmful thoughts. In effect, it changes the perception of ourselves from a victim who continues to wish that the past would be different to one who is empowered to see hope in the future. We cannot change the past, but we can change our perception of it and release ourselves from bitterness. We alter our perceptions by seeing that our partner operated out of fear or pain and did not know how to handle emotions. If we so choose, we can work things out and revive the feelings of love. Or we can decide that it is best to dissolve the union and forgive ourselves for any part we played. The path to forgiveness is a process. Leonard guides his clients through a step-by-step process incorporating three R's: **Recognize** the distress; **Release** the pain; and **Resolve** the issues.

RECOGNIZE

The first step is to recognize any pain or resentment associated with ourselves, another person, or an event. Our negative emotions may show themselves in sarcasm, revenge, physical pain like headaches, passive-aggressive behaviors, or outright hostility. When we recognize our distress, we become aware of feeling fear, anger, or sadness, as well as disturbing thoughts associated with the emotions. We may ask ourselves if we feel victimized, controlled, or disrespected. This recognition begins our transformation.

If there is an area of our life that needs forgiveness, it will be triggered by actions or words of those closest to us. The poet Rumi said, "The wound is the place where the light enters you." In other words, any neglect, abandonment, or abuse from our childhood will inevitably be triggered by something our lover says or does that reminds us of an old hurt. If we are mindful of painful emotions, we can face them head-on.

Recognizing old wounds is a wake-up call, asking us to acknowledge what causes us pain so we can express ourselves, set boundaries, and release the painful emotions. As with any healing, we must first diagnose the source of our dis-ease. Forgiving people who have hurt us and recognizing the link to our present circumstances move us forward to give and receive love fully. We can recognize any disturbance more clearly by asking the following questions:

1. What caused me to feel upset?

When angry or frustrated with our partner, we can ask ourselves what happened, who did what, and why we felt offended or victimized. It is important to spend some time listening to ourselves or writing down our thoughts without attacking, defending, or judging. We often have an expectation that our partner should behave in a certain way. When that doesn't occur, we may react negatively, thinking we are disrespected, attacked, victimized, or unloved. Answering the question in this step may reveal our internal negative story.

> Joan: *Stan never cleans up after himself in the kitchen. I constantly have to pick up after him. He is insensitive and selfish.*

2. What am I feeling about what happened?

In this step, we give ourselves permission to acknowledge emotions of anger, fear, and sadness. We focus inward, avoiding attacking, defending, or judging ourselves. Our feelings about the situation need to be exposed to the light so we can understand them. This process often involves grieving a loss such as trust, respect, or intimacy. Although we may be tempted to mask our feelings, we can't heal what we can't see or allow ourselves to feel, so honestly answering this question exposes suppressed emotions.

> Joan: *I get so mad when I see his dirty dishes in the sink. I feel like a doormat. I fume inside so when Stan asks for a hug, I tell him I'm too tired.*

3. What is the payoff for me to hold onto these feelings?

This may be hard to spot. However, when we hold onto negative emotions, there is usually some reward and a cost. The payoff may be feelings of self-righteousness or revenge. Holding on to angry feelings may be familiar and change can be more frightening than the fear of addressing them. We may hope to avoid conflict or even believe that keeping the painful feelings within will make them disappear. The cost of hiding emotions is an erected wall that separates us from our lover. When we stop communicating and hold onto resentment, we stifle our ability to connect.

> Joan: *If Stan doesn't help me around the house, I don't have to feel guilty about being tired and not wanting sex. I can fantasize about making love with someone who cherishes me.*

RELEASE

Once we recognize our thoughts and feelings, and why we have held onto them, we can move toward the next step to let them go. Releasing requires a shift in our thinking and behavior, not always the easiest to do, especially when emotions are intense. That's why we must calm ourselves to be able to think more clearly about what is most important to us. We will focus on the following ways to release unforgiving thoughts and pain: centering the body; reframing thoughts; journaling; implementing rituals; and/or working with a counselor.

1. Centering the body

Have you ever let off some steam, had a good cry, laughed in your belly, or experienced a pulsating orgasm? Fritz Perls, who created Gestalt therapy, stated that there were four ways that the body released energy through catharsis—anger, sadness, laughter, and orgasm. Releasing pent-up emotions can shift our energy so we don't get stuck in them.

If we have a difficulty expressing anger or sadness or we explode, it may be helpful to center ourselves and connect with our body and emotions as a way to release them. We can tense our muscles and say, "I feel the anger in my shoulders," then relax and release the tension while saying, "I now let go." Tensing and relaxing the muscles trains the body to let go of unwanted stress. Other forms of physical release such as exercise, yoga, deep breathing, laughing, or orgasm alters the chemicals in the body and produces neurotransmitters and hormones that make us feel good. They help shift the energy to a place where we don't feel overwhelmed.

Slow deep breaths relax us. It focuses our attention within so we can be mindful of the present moment. Taking deep breaths into the diaphragm, we simultaneously tell ourselves to breathe in calm, then exhale and let go of anger or any other negative emotion. In the process, we may find ourselves yawning. Research shows that deliberate yawning immediately calms the brain and centers the body. Consciously breathing and yawning makes us more serene and receptive to releasing anything that causes us agitation or distress. With a centered physical body and a calm mind, we have the ability to create new thoughts to reframe the past.

2. Reframing thoughts

When we look at a situation, we tend to peer through our own frame of reference. We believe our point of view is true for everyone. Our thought framework determines how we see the world. We create a story in our mind that gives meaning to every experience. That story plays out in our relationships. If we felt unloved as a child, we will replay that same story like a movie. The story is merely our narrative about our life experiences. As long as we look through the same frame of reference, we will have the same story with the same outcome. We need to remember that our loved one has his/her own different perception of reality based on his/her life story.

When we look at a situation from a different perspective, we alter our frame of reference, and we change our view. If we look up instead of down, we see a different world. Instead of perceiving our partner as an enemy, we can question why he/she reacts in a particular manner. Before assuming our partner's intent, we can become curious about their reasons for acting or speaking in a particular manner. That sense of curiosity helps us gain insight into their past and recognize the hurt inner child who longs for love. We each do the best we can with the relationship tools that we have learned. If we knew better, we would do better. Reframing our thoughts to consider alternate viewpoints shifts our focus away from condemning our partner's way of thinking. If we can mentally step into their shoes, we gain insight into why he or she acted in a particular manner that was hurtful.

Ask this question to reframe your partner's actions. What might be the reason, other than to hurt me, for my partner to act the way he or she did?

This step is more challenging because we now try to understand why our loved one has hurt us. We acknowledge him/her as a human being and step into his/her shoes as best as we can. With an attitude of compassion, we see our partner as a human being who is fallible just like us and may be using old ineffective strategies to get their needs met.

> Joan: *Stan isn't purposely trying to irritate me by not washing the dishes. He doesn't realize why it's so important to me. He has a higher tolerance for mess and gets angry when I bring it up. I like the house to be neat and tidy. That makes me feel happier. I know that when Stan was a little boy, his parents were critical and unappreciative every time he did something. I believe he loves me because he shows it in other ways, like bringing me flowers and being affectionate.*

3. Journaling

Many years ago, Leonard worked with a depressed woman in her thirties who had a rare, debilitating illness. Growing up, she was raised in an abusive household and kept to herself. She believed she was stupid, ugly, and without much hope for the future. She could barely express herself verbally. That negatively impacted her marriage.

Leonard asked her to write a few thoughts in a journal in between therapy sessions and bring them so he could read them. Her first entry was one sentence, illegibly scribbled on a crumpled piece of paper, "I don't like myself."

Over time, she brought in her journal at the beginning of each session. Her simple sentences soon turned into paragraphs, releasing her pain. Ultimately, her pages blossomed into completed journals.

As her writing expanded, so did her life. She grew in confidence and became more verbally expressive with her husband and with others. She founded a support group for individuals with the rare disability, started a newsletter, and built a remarkable organization that connected families who were affected by the disability. In essence, she created a supportive, loving extended family by forgiving the past and releasing the negative thoughts through her journals. The changes all began because of the power of words.

The late Maya Angelou used writing to liberate herself, so beautifully expressed in her book, *I Know Why the Caged Bird Sings*. Her words acted as keys that unlocked the doors to forgiveness.

Journaling is a wonderful vehicle to express our thoughts and feelings without worrying about what others think. The journal becomes our own private therapist who listens and welcomes our words. It allows us to release any wounds and bitterness to identify what we need and desire. We don't need to share what we write with anyone else, unless we want to. We just write about anything that comes to mind so that we release the hidden emotions and bring them into the light where they are less frightening.

When Mari was in the throes of her divorce many years ago, she wrote in her journal every night after her children went to sleep. She released pent-up emotions and clarified what she wanted in life. After the divorce was over, she spent a weekend reading what she had written. She recognized the many stages of grieving and forgiveness that she went through. She then shredded the pages and placed them into the fireplace to burn away the agony and sadness so she could metaphorically rise like the phoenix out of the ashes. Now she recommends to all her clients that they journal as they go through the process of mediation.

Some choose to keep their journals; others prefer to burn the pages like Mari. She incorporated another form of releasing—rituals.

4. Rituals

Letting go and forgiveness sometimes calls for a ritual. Rituals are part of our lives. We may have a morning ritual of reading the newspaper and drinking a cup of coffee, meditating, walking, reading spiritual material, or checking email. We have rituals for rites of passage such as a Bar and Bat Mitzvah, wedding, or memorial service. They provide meaning to our lives and help us with transitions. Marriage traditionally begins with a ceremony before a group of witnesses to mark the beginning of a couple's life together. That ritual reinforces a commitment, "Till death do we part."

While rituals reinforce behaviors, they can also help release unwanted emotions and thoughts. When Mari created a ritual to burn her journal, it was her way of releasing the past to make changes in her life. She opened herself to eventually meet her soul mate and husband, Lloyd.

Rituals such as lighting a candle before a couple holds a conversation about a problem indicates a desire to hold each other in the light. This reminds them to seek the highest good for one another.

Another forgiveness ritual, called Ho'oponopono, was popularized by Dr. Hew Len, a psychologist who worked on a ward for the criminally insane in a Hawaiian State Hospital. He used the Hawaiian healing process on the patients with incredible results. The ward eventually closed down because the patients were healed. He used four simple statements that he repeated over and over in his mind:

I am sorry.

Please forgive me.

I love you.

Thank you.

While this ritual sounds simple, it is a powerful way to break through resentments and move toward deep healing. A number of years ago, while Leonard was in Chicago, he took the opportunity to invite his ex-wife, Marylou, to attend his Roadmap Home seminar. At the time, they had been divorced fourteen years after a long marriage of twenty-six years.

Over the years, the stinging memories of the painful divorce began to melt like a spring thaw. During the seminar, Leonard asked participants to move into pairs and identify areas of healing that needed forgiveness. Each person then used the Ho'oponopono ritual with one another. Leonard paired with Marylou and openly expressed sorrow and forgiveness, poignant moments for both of them.

Several days later, Leonard and Marylou had dinner at her place. They talked further about the ending of their marriage and found that even after fourteen years of being apart, there was room for additional healing.

Marylou found her wedding ring and decided to release it into water, a spontaneous ritual of emotional release and flow. The small lake outside her condominium beckoned the sterling silver wedding band.

At 10:30 that night, they walked to the wooden bridge that crossed the lake near Marylou's residence. She said a prayer and tossed the wedding ring into the water as a final goodbye gesture. When the ring splashed beneath the surface, a miracle occurred. The overhead lights of the bridge flashed on like a Christmas tree. Leonard and Marylou both stared at each other in amazement as if the universe said, "It's about time you both lightened up."

As they crossed the bridge, they recalled a song that was popular during their courtship by Simon and Garfunkel, "Bridge Over Troubled Water." Hollywood couldn't have set the scene any better!

Letting go of past hurts opens us to healing. With forgiveness, Leonard and Marylou moved past the hurt toward acceptance and inner peace. When Marylou passed away several years later, Leonard was grateful for the positive closure they experienced before her passing.

A ritual of forgiveness carries us across the bridge over troubled waters. It takes courage and an intention to let go of the hurt and anger and open our heart to joyful liberation.

RESOLVE

Oprah Winfrey once said, "True forgiveness is when you can say, 'Thank you for that experience.'" That sums up the phase of resolution where we have integrated what we learned and arrived at a place of inner peace. We have resolved the conflict and have established a deeper connection with our partner. Our hearts have opened, and we have expanded our capacity to be compassionate, understanding, and loving.

When we resolve an issue, we find a deeper meaning to our lives and our story. The following questions can help you experience resolution.

1. How might I see this as something I need to learn?

The self-help author and speaker Wayne Dyer once said, "You will see it when you believe it." We can shift our perception so that we view what happened as a plan for our growth. Our purpose on this earth is to learn lessons and deal with issues and evolve. Therefore, we can look for the lessons that we need to learn. A crucial lesson is to let go of debilitating unforgiving emotions that hold us back. Forgiveness propels us further on our journey of life lessons.

> Joan: *I can be very judgmental with Stan, especially when he doesn't do what I want him to do. My lesson is to learn to accept who he is and to be grateful for all that we share together.*

2. What am I supposed to do with this growth?

We become empowered in this stage because we no longer accept the role of the victim. We have reframed the old story of our perceptions about the past hurts and recognized that our soul needed to experience the pain to become more conscious of what we need to change. Rather than seeing past conflict as a horrible obstacle that we must replay in our heads, we now view it as an opportunity to heal and create a healthier relationship. We take responsibility for our emotions, our viewpoints, and our commitment to forgive, knowing that each challenge is merely a life lesson. The greater the challenge, the greater the reward when we forgive.

The act of forgiveness is our salvation, because it not only brings meaning to our lives but also inner peace. We can share that realization with our partner, thereby enriching the relationship. We connect at a deeper level when we grow and learn from each other.

> Joan: *Instead of shutting down, I commit to practicing forgiveness with Stan. I plan to relieve myself of the*

chains of resentment and open my heart to love. I plan to communicate how I feel without blaming, criticizing, or judging him. I recognize his need to be appreciated, and I will be more grateful.

There may be times when you may not feel like you can completely forgive. It is a process of working toward total letting go of the bitterness of situations. If you need to vent first, you could say in your mind or in your journal, "I forgive you, you damn..." As you release the emotions, the anger may shift to sadness and eventually to genuine forgiveness.

A lack of inner peace or a tinge of pain or anger is a clear indication that you have further work. If that is the case, recycle back to the initial step of recognition. Asking yourself the questions several times will help you forgive a deep wound that needs to be brought into the light and released. Traumatic injuries of childhood or from former relationships take time and patience to uncover and release. But remember, you are not forgiving others for them, but rather for you so you can be rid of the agony.

If you need help moving through these steps, consider working with a therapist who provides a safe healing space where you can experience true forgiveness. When you let go of anguish from the past, you allow yourself to feel freedom to be cared for and loved. From that place of self-acceptance, you have more love to give yourself and receive from your partner.

FIGHTING FOR LOVE EXERCISES:

1. Choose an incident where you felt hurt by your partner. When you think of the incident, what emotional and physical feelings arise?

2. What could be the emotional payoff for holding onto those feelings?

3. What might be the reason, other than to hurt you, for your partner to act the way he or she did?

4. How might you see this experience as something you need to learn?

5. What will you do differently in the future?

Forgiveness does not change the past,
but it does enlarge the future.

– Paul Boese

"Same-sex marriage is nothing new.
We've been having the same sex for 25 years."

CHAPTER 9

Change Your Thinking;
Change Your Love Life

---

*"Your life mainly consists of three things:
what you think, what you say, and what
you do. So always be very conscious of your
choices and what you are co-creating!"*

— Allan Rufus

Adam and Steven had been loving partners for ten years. They wanted to connect at a deep soul level, but they became defensive when one or the other brought up a problem or unmet need. After several frustrating years, they decided it was time to move on.

Working with Mari in mediation, the couple recognized that neither of them had explored their individual contributions to the breakdown of the relationship. During the process, Adam and Steven began to assess what each did that escalated the conflict. During mediation, they admitted that they needed to be more conscious of their thoughts, change their tone, and eliminate blame. Both wanted love, respect, caring, and understanding. This honest sharing made them realize that they could collaborate together and feel understood. They decided to fight for love and give their relationship another chance.

In Chapter 3, we talked about clarifying your needs and desires with your partner. When your needs are unmet, conflict grabs your attention so you can move toward satisfying those needs. If you have told your partner about those needs, but feel they have been ignored, or if you haven't asked for what you desired because you believed your partner should know what you want, you can choose to fight for love.

Whenever you have conflict in your love relationship, you have four choices: you can end the relationship, accept being miserable, negotiate for change, or change yourself.

1. End the Relationship

If you have engaged in counseling or mediation, and the acrimony continued to escalate, you can leave temporarily from a joint living situation or end the relationship. If you have endured continual conflict, taking a break from each other while both are in therapy may provide a new perspective and insight.

You learn and grow in relationships. However, if the situation continues to be painful, even after trying various tools and remedies, you may choose wisely by ending an unhealthy, toxic union. If you do choose to end a relationship that is not working, you can do it with dignity and respect without blame. Releasing criticism and guilt, while acknowledging the good in both of you, helps the two of you move on. A breakup becomes a healthier learning experience when you recognize that you both played a part. You may have learned all that you can from a partnership that was not meant to last forever.

2. Accept Misery as a Choice

If you are willing to look within yourself, you will recognize that unhappiness is a *choice*. You have volunteered to stay and, therefore, you are not a victim. You may have allowed the situation to persist by not confronting the issues. If you continue to do what you've always done, you'll continue to get the same results. You may be stuck. Once you realize this, consider changing yourself and negotiating for a positive change.

3. Negotiate for Change

Negotiation necessitates a willingness to hear the concerns from your partner without defensiveness. You each show respect and understanding by listening and mirroring back what you have heard without judgment. It demonstrates to your partner that you are attentive and open to listening without interruption so you can problem solve as a team. The next chapter offers specific steps to help you to do this successfully.

4. Change Yourself

Even though there are three other choices, whether it is ending the relationship, accepting being miserable, or negotiating for change, we believe that changing ourselves empowers us to manage our lives. When we admit that we have responsibility for the part we play in the conflict and are prepared to alter our approach, we can change the relationship and reignite positive feelings, even passion.

Couples who come in for counseling or mediation usually have an agenda — they want to change their partner. Someone in conflict usually thinks, "It's not me, it's you!" However, this position creates a power struggle as two people engage in a win/lose battle to convince the other that they are the problem. This strategy emphasizes separation rather than togetherness. It also places the power into the hands of another: "If only she/he will act differently, I will be happy." That position means that happiness comes from the outside.

How do you change your thinking? Say to yourself, "It's not you, it's me." You may immediately recoil at that phrase, believing that doing so means you are to blame. Saying "It's me" asks that you take responsibility for your own attitudes, judgments, and actions by becoming aware of how you think. You can examine your part of the problem and recognize what you bring from your childhood and previous partners into your current relationship. As you analyze how you can change yourself to be happier, you willingly take positive steps to alter your thinking. You can even adopt an attitude of gratitude for the fact that you are improving yourself.

Ask yourself these questions:

- If it's me, what part do I play in creating conflict?

- How do I criticize or judge myself or my loved one?

- What am I doing that I did as a child or when I was with a previous partner that no longer serves me?

- How can I overcome my tendency to withdraw or engage in battle so that I can create more love in my life?

- How can I become more mindful of my thoughts?

MINDFULNESS CREATES ATTENTION AND INTENTION

Observing our thoughts, letting go of the past, and stopping ourselves from ruminating about the future enables us to live in the now. Actually, the present is all we have. We can be aware of the past for what it taught us, but we don't have to stay there. We can distract ourselves with technology and TV, or we can commit to accepting life as it is and making constructive changes in our thinking.

Our thoughts define who we are. We are either consciously or unconsciously creating our lives and our relationships. When we live unconsciously, we do not control who we are or what we hope to bring into our lives. We then become victims of outer circumstances.

With mindfulness, we become observers of our thoughts, actions, behaviors, and attitudes. We deliberately choose what we desire in our relationship with ourselves and our loved ones. We can't control outer circumstances or how our loved one thinks or acts; however, we do have the power to manage our thoughts and emotions so they don't take over and rule us.

With mindfulness, we pay attention to how we think moment by moment, without judgment, without analyzing the past or fearing the future. Once we attend to our thinking, we can respond to our emotions and the emotions of others. We don't have to be slaves to negative thoughts. Positive and negative emotions are triggered in the brain by thoughts, which are often unconscious. As we become aware of them, we can choose calmness over agitation, acceptance over judgment, and optimism over pessimism.

Mari's former professor, William Ury, Harvard negotiations professor and author of *Getting to Yes with Yourself and Other Worthy Opponents*, wrote, "A key to staying in the present moment I have learned is to be able to focus on what lasts while accepting what passes... By focusing on what is lasting — life itself, nature, the universe — we become more aware of what is passing, more appreciative of the preciousness and temporary nature of every experience. In turn, as we become more aware that these experiences won't last forever, we become less reactive in situations of conflict — after all, whatever the conflict is, this too shall pass — and we find it easier to look for the present opportunity to get to yes with others."[8]

One way to bring yourself into the present moment is to focus on your breathing. When you feel an intense emotion, pay attention to your breath — both

---

8   Ury, William, *Getting to Yes with Yourself and Other Worthy Opponents*, New York: HarperOne, 2015; pp. 111/112.

the inhalation and the exhalation. Doing this may ease any tension. By placing your awareness on what is happening now, you calm your mind. You can then seize the opportunity to create a clear intention of how you want to think. Greater clarity gives you the power to change your thinking and shift your attitude so you can improve the way you relate with your loved one.

Let's try an exercise. Become mindful right now and pay attention to your breathing. Feel how your abdomen expands as you inhale. Notice the warm air exiting from your nostrils as you exhale. Notice the tempo of inhaling and exhaling. Do this several times. Now consider that at one time you chose to love your partner. Return to an early memory when you first met. Ask these three questions:

- Where were you?

- What were you doing when you fell in love?

- How did you feel?

Most likely, you felt happy and joyful with the thrill of a touch. Remember the fun you had together. This mere suggestion may catapult you back to the past. For a brief moment, picture yourself happy in the relationship. Allow your feelings to expand throughout your body. Now notice that you effortlessly changed your thoughts.

Every day we have anywhere between 50,000 and 75,000 thoughts. Any discord between you and your loved one is based on your thoughts. You can transform your thinking and your approach to any conflict. Choosing a different perspective causes you to act differently and, ultimately, change the situation. Thus, if you think and behave differently, your partner will probably respond in a new way. But beware: when you change, your partner may try to get you to react as you had before, because the old patterns are more familiar and, in an odd way, more comfortable. However, if you remain consistent and persist in your new positive attitude and actions, eventually you'll notice a positive shift in your lover's reaction.

Try another experiment. During a time of conflict, avoid becoming defensive, angry, critical, or reactive to anything negative your partner says. Instead, pause, then take slow, deep breaths and imagine a golden shield protecting you from any verbal attacks or criticism. Watch any thoughts that rise to the surface. Immediately replace negative ones with neutral or positive thoughts. For example, if your lover tells you that you are a lousy driver, a terrible cook, or a horrible lover, take a moment to breathe slowly. Tell yourself that your partner is sharing his or her feelings about an unmet need. It may or may not be about you. You can be curious about what your partner needs. This could take you to a place of understanding rather than judgment.

When a person acts in a nasty manner, it usually means he or she is feeling negative about himself or herself. You don't have to respond in kind. Pause and regain your composure. Then ask your partner in a gentle, curious tone, "Help me understand why you said that?" Avoid attacking or becoming defensive, although you may feel like lashing out. Be inquisitive. You are not agreeing with what was said, but rather are wondering why it was said. If you stay centered without getting furious or reacting to the criticism, you and your loved one can open the door to connection.

As you remain conscious about how you are thinking and feeling, notice what pushes your buttons. You can then stop yourself from fighting back or fleeing and ask open-ended questions to find out more. Then listen, reframe the negative statement, and ask for clarification.

Here's an example of a couple driving toward potential conflict, where one partner consciously steers the conversation toward a positive outcome:

Anna: *You're a lousy driver!*

John: (In a neutral tone) *I heard you say that I'm not a good driver. Tell me specifically what you mean.*

Anna: *You drive too slow when you're in the fast lane.*

John: *I'm worried about getting a speeding ticket. Would you be more comfortable if I drove in the middle lane?*

Anna: *I'd rather have you drive faster so we get there before tomorrow. But, yeah, it would be better if you drove in the middle lane. I don't want to have an accident.*

John: *Thanks for letting me know. I'll move over so you can feel safe. I don't want you to be scared.*

Anna: *Honey, I'm sorry I yelled at you.*

In the scenario above, John did not react to Anna's attacks, but responded to the underlying issue of both parties wanting to be safe. If John had reacted angrily, the conversation could have turned into an intense argument that would have been more dangerous than driving too slowly in the fast lane.

By changing our approach from defensive or offensive to neutral, an explosive situation can be averted. It takes focus and concentration not to react defensively when we feel attacked. Volatile reactions never get us what we want. When we respond neutrally, we retain our power, dignity, and grace. A win/lose contest means one partner ends up a loser. Both can be winners. It only takes one to detach from the negative emotions and redirect the conversation toward a positive outcome. If our partner pushes us to the point of anger, we lose our power and self-control.

Before you blame your partner over an argument, ask yourself if you would rather be right than happy? If you feel it's important to win every argument no matter the circumstance, you choose to let your ego and anger rule. When that happens, resolving issues is unlikely. There are no winners when you engage in the blame game.

If, however, your mature mindful self takes charge, you can say, "It's not my partner, it's me." That will remind you to listen respectfully. You can deflect the acrimony and hear and understand each other and reunite peacefully.

Everyone makes mistakes. Learning from them creates wisdom. Your love relationship will soar when you own your part and consciously change your thinking and actions. If you consistently raise your voice, attack, offend, demand, refuse to discuss issues, or nag your partner, you can replace those unproductive tactics with more effective approaches.

If you are fed up with your relationship and do not feel motivated to make changes in yourself, but would rather just end it, ask yourself how leaving will resolve your part of the problem. Not recognizing that you are partially at fault prevents you from making changes in yourself. You don't have to wait until you leave a relationship. You will take your patterns with you wherever you go. A new partner may look different and seem a better fit at first, but after a while, unresolved conflicts will eventually reappear. Whatever you resist seeing in yourself will persist and cause similar pain, until you change your thinking and transform your way of dealing with difficult issues.

By analyzing our behaviors and actively listening to our partner's feedback about what doesn't work, we can make better choices about how we wish to respond in tense situations. For example, if our partner complained about not having enough time together, we can either take it as criticism, or we can appreciate our partner for wanting to be with us. If our partner points out controlling behavior, we can get angry and defensive. Alternately, we can question our own actions, ask for feedback, and learn to let go of what doesn't work. As our perception shifts from criticism to appreciation, so will our relationship.

Refocus on positive, appreciative thoughts and choose an attitude of gratitude. Create a thank-you list for everything small and large that your loved one does for you. Ask for what you *do* want and avoid complaining about what you don't want. Be conscious of all the good things that your lover does, and show your gratitude. Even if your partner complains about the way you look, ask for clarification about what could be improved. Instead of getting mad, be grateful for the opportunity to look better.

Try the following experiment. For a whole day, identify all that you appreciate about your partner. Then, using a positive tone, share your appreciations throughout the day. Send a text or email, make a phone call, or give your partner a card. Focus on appreciations, even during frustrating interactions. You can thank you partner for taking the kids to school, cleaning the garage, paying the bills, making dinner, even making love! Share your gratitude.

During a counseling session, Leonard heard Timothy constantly complain about Sharon's messy habits. They were driving him crazy. The kitchen was never clean, the laundry was backed up, and the house was untidy. Whatever Sharon did, Timothy turned it into a complaint. Leonard asked him if he was always so negative.

"Only after I married Sharon!" he grumbled.

"So before you were with Sharon, you were positive, and after Sharon, you became negative. Is that right?" asked Leonard.

"Yes."

"So how do you see the way your mind works?"

Timothy said, "My mind is very organized."

"Since your mind is so organized, you will have no trouble helping Sharon change. And I know you want Sharon to change."

Timothy nodded in agreement. "I want her to be more organized like me."

"You can help Sharon by demonstrating how to change. Are you up for the challenge?"

"Sure, what do I have to do?"

Leonard then instructed Timothy to point out only the positive behaviors about Sharon during the week. If he saw a messy kitchen, he would praise her for cooking a lovely meal. If he saw an untidy room, he could tidy it up himself. When Sharon noticed that he helped, he would be grateful about her appreciation. Timothy believed that since he was organized and focused, he could easily focus on positives for a week.

At the next counseling session, Sharon walked in beaming. Timothy, on the other hand, sheepishly admitted that it was hard to focus on the positives. He didn't realize how much he complained. He also had to admit the good news. As a result of showing Sharon appreciation, she became more loving and even approached Timothy for sex. They both decided on cleaning the house together and enjoyed one another.

Here's another experiment. For one week, focus on saying *please* and *thank you* for verbal exchanges whenever you make a request of your loved one. Consciously use a gentle loving voice, even if you are frustrated with a situation. Look at your partner with a kind face. Notice what happens and how you feel about your partner's reactions.

For example, "Honey, could you please take the dog out." If your partner satisfies the request, say, "Thank you. I really appreciate you doing this."

As we stay aware of the present, not thinking about yesterday's problems or tomorrow's concerns, we become more available for what's happening in the relationship. We discover that we have the power to make a positive difference. Our choices and our changes are gifts for the growth and the evolution of our relationship.

We can acknowledge that we have done the best we could in the past. We can acquire new tools and lovingly alter our approach, thus transforming our relationship.

Once you commit to working on yourself, the next step is to make a conscious effort to negotiate for mutual changes. In the next chapter, we share strategies to help you and your partner find solutions to problems and get what you desire.

FIGHTING FOR LOVE EXERCISES:

To help you change your thinking, answer the following questions:

1. When you and your loved one argue, what part do you play in escalating the conflict?

    a. When are you judgmental, blaming, or controlling?
    b. How do you see yourself in the relationship? Are you accepting, forgiving, and loving?

2. Take a notebook and write down all that is positive about being in your relationship.

3. Make a list of your positive attributes on one side of a paper. On the other side, make a list of your partner's positive attributes.

4. Share them with your partner.

5. What three things can you do to make positive changes in yourself to resolve conflict? For example, you can actively listen without interruption or gently ask open-ended questions. Share with each other your willingness to make the changes.

"We're looking for something to fix our
marriage. I'm in Barnes & Noble,
he's in Home Depot."

CHAPTER 10

What's the Solution?
Make Me a Deal.

You never really understand a person until you consider things from his point of view...until you climb into his skin and walk around in it.

— Atticus Finch, *To Kill a Mockingbird*

Deanna and Brian, both lawyers, thought they knew how to resolve their marriage issues. After all, they negotiated every day in their careers. But when they tried to bargain with each other, as they did with their legal cases, about who was at fault, who had the advantage, and who could out-argue the other, they hit a wall. Positional bargaining didn't work with love issues. In mediation, the couple had to unlearn the old ways of arguing to win and empower themselves with interest-based solutions to get fair, mutually satisfying agreements. Instead of proving who was right, they needed to focus on common interests and the future.

When we have a breakdown in communication, conflict is a signal that it is time to negotiate for change. In the business world, people often think negotiation must include tricks, tactics, and game-playing which may only work, if at all, in the short term. But that approach never works for healthy relationships. Mutual bargaining, which benefits everyone, also works well in the business world. It is the most effective way for us to meet one another's needs and boost our connection. We satisfy our underlying interests by cooperating, conciliating, and making mutual promises, which we keep.

Mari created the term "solutioneering" instead of problem solving to help her clients in disputes focus on positive solutions, rather than blaming for past wrongs. The shift in thinking from *problem* to *solution* frames the approach as an opportunity to collaborate and reach mutually satisfying agreements.

As we search for solutions as a team, we give our loved one the gift of listening, understanding, and acceptance. We create an optimistic process to support and negotiate with each other for change. Rather than forcing change or converting the other person to our way of thinking, we share our reasoning and brainstorm favorable results to meet mutual interests toward a resolution.

In the earlier example, Deanna and Brian had to transform their thinking from winning an argument and preparing a response while the other was speaking, to listening and understanding their partner's feelings and concerns. Brian and Deanna learned to actively listen to one another and to neutrally mirror back what the other said. That wasn't easy for the two lawyers. That feeling of being heard motivated them to collaborate together and avoid a battle.

When we reflect back what we hear from each other, we become open to learn from each other. Focusing on our partner's words, tone, and body movement to catch the essence of what was said provides us with insight into their thoughts, feelings, and underlying needs. Taking notes can help us keep track of our partner's point of view. Mari prefers note taking during her mediation sessions to assure that she will remember the key points. Even when solutioneering with her husband Lloyd, they both take notes to insure they don't miss important issues. It also helps them be nonjudgmental and focus on what is being said so they can manage their emotions. On the other hand, Leonard deals with clients as a therapist and prefers that a couple maintain direct eye contact during their interactions. This helps some communicate directly with their partner and resist the temptation to prepare a rebuttal. Even in his personal relationships, Leonard prefers face-to-face contact when dealing with issues.

If you do take notes, Mari suggests that when writing, you pause to maintain eye contact and watch the facial and body language, so you don't miss critical cues. If issues are complex, writing them down can bring clarity, but remember to look at each other to build rapport. The brain only absorbs a limited amount at a time, so if you do not take notes, reflect back to your partner in short sentences throughout the discussion to demonstrate that you are listening and you understand.

To keep a challenging conversation positive, we need to reframe negative statements or accusations and use non-offensive words to bring the communication to a more harmonious level. This is clarified in the steps below.

SOLUTIONEERING: Your Strategy for Negotiating Loving Agreements

1. Identify a concern and plan a meeting with your partner.

Whether you have an issue about money, children, sex, or any other issue, you will feel better once you address the issues in a gentle and calm manner. Speaking to concerns when they arise clears the air and enables you to jointly strategize for a happier future. If you are the one who has a concern, request a time to talk with your partner. Don't say you want to focus on a problem. Instead, ask your partner for a time to sit together calmly and discuss how things are going. Set the meeting when there will be no interruptions. Turn off the television and smartphones! You may want to put on calming music to set the mood. Allow at least fifteen to twenty minutes. Bring a pen and notebook, or your tablet or iPad if you want to take notes.

Before you attend the meeting, consider some positive things you can say to your partner about the relationship. Jot down some ideas to focus on how you could solve the issue of concern, keeping in mind your partner's interests. Plan to use "I" Messages and avoid blaming or criticizing your loved one.

Resist the temptation to bring out a host of issues, be defensive, or change the subject. Select one area of the concern that is the least inflammatory or complex. Your problem-solving process will be more successful if you start solutioneering with easier issues. Picture a positive resolution with the discussion moving toward what you want, *not* what you don't want.

Here is an example of a young couple, Kathy and Jordan, who are so busy they rarely have time to connect.

Kathy's issue was that she wanted Jordan to spend more time with her and the children. Kathy felt like telling Jordan, "You're selfish. You work too damn much and never spend quality time with me and the kids. And you're too tired to make love." Instead, she only focused on her desire for more time with him.

From Jordan's perspective, he wanted appreciation. He could have said, "You're always nagging me and don't appreciate all that I do for you and the kids." Instead, he identified his issue of feeling stressed to earn enough money for the family so he could spend more time with them.

The couple identified the challenge of the lack of quality time (Kathy's issue) versus appreciation for providing for the family (Jordan's issue). Their goal was to meet each other's interests.

2. Start your discussion with gratitude and a positive statement.

Meet in a nonthreatening place and establish a comfortable, pleasing atmosphere. Finger food and a beverage might help you "break bread together." Soft music soothes the soul. Start off a difficult conversation with words of appreciation. Thank your partner for taking the time to meet together. Then state a positive statement about him/her or the relationship, such as, "I'm grateful that we can work through challenges as a team." Sincerely give your loved one a sense of security that this will be a loving exchange of ideas. Speak slowly and in soft tone of voice.

In this scenario, both parties were coached through the process. Kathy thanked Jordan for taking the children to the baseball game and told him how much she appreciated his hard work. Jordan thanked Kathy for caring for the children and being invested in the relationship.

3. Calmly bring up a concern that you have without finding fault.

Avoid the temptation to leap into a problem with fingers pointing, saying, "You are the problem, not me!" Blaming raises the defenses and counterattacks. Frame the issue in a way that allows for a solution. If there is a financial problem, the intention can be to improve finances. "We are both concerned about money. How can we jointly reduce our expenses and increase our savings?" If the problem is one of communication, frame it as a desire to be honest, open, and more intimate. "Let's brainstorm how we can speak to each other in a way so we both feel heard and respected?"

4. Actively listen and reflect back what you heard.

Active listening involves an intention to pay close attention to what is being said, comprehend the meaning, and reflect it back. Deep listening includes engaging body language and maintaining eye contact. Nodding one's head or saying "hmm" can also convey an attitude of paying attention. In *Keeping the Love You Find*, Harville Hendrix mentions a threefold process of listening that includes mirroring, validating, and empathy.

We all have a need to be heard and understood. We can become so intent on responding defensively that we may focus more on proving our point than hearing our partner. Be respectful, don't interrupt, and tenderly look at your partner, even if he/she says something that pushes your buttons. If you take notes to remember what is being said, frequently look at your partner to maintain eye contact with a positive attitude. Agree that you will both listen without interrupting until your partner has finished. The more you listen, the more you will understand. Your reflective response will show your partner that you recognize his/her perspective.

Each can remind the other that the discussion is not about who is right or wrong. Listen actively without judgment or defensiveness. To do this, you may need to take slow, deep breaths and concentrate on staying calm. If you appear aggressive or defensive, your body language will escalate the conflict. Even if you don't agree, remember that your partner has a right to view situations and life differently. Listening without arguing doesn't mean that you acquiesce to the other person's point of view. Rather, you convey respect and love when you are relaxed and open to hearing your loved one's point of view.

When you reflect back what your partner has said, you demonstrate caring and understanding. You give your partner an opportunity to be validated. If you don't capture the total essence of what was said, ask your partner to clarify the issue or say it differently. When your loved one hears you calmly mirror back what you heard and sees that you are not reacting defensively, he or she will become less defensive and more open to reciprocate. Maintaining your composure will help you both stay on track toward resolving issues. If either one of you gets angry, take some deep breaths. If necessary, take a break so you can calm down before resuming.

As you both listen attentively, you will recognize emotions, thoughts, and behaviors that either block or enhance your positive connection. Recognizing erroneous assumptions about what your partner was thinking enables you to see options for a mutual agreement.

In the scenario with Kathy and Jordan, Kathy used an "I" Message to ask for what she wanted instead of a blaming "You" Message for what she didn't want.

Kathy: *The kids and I miss you. I would love more time with you so we can enjoy time as a family.*

Jordan: *I hear that you wish I would spend more time with you and the kids. Did I understand you correctly?*

With coaching, he did not react defensively with, "Don't nag me." Instead, he reflected back her concerns.

Kathy: *Yes. I just don't feel we're connecting anymore.*

Jordan: *I recognize that we don't see each other much, and you feel that we are not connecting. You and the kids are very important to me.*

He repeated what was said without being defensive. He then added a sentence to show empathy, understanding, and encouragement.

Kathy: *You're important to me too. I want to work this out.*

She felt legitimized, understood, and cared for.

5. Take turns stating your needs and concerns.

Establish a process of giving and receiving as you take turns asking for what you would like to happen or what you would like from your partner. Avoid any criticism about the past and positively focus on the present. Suggest how you both can improve the situation together. Make the discussion a joint collaboration to arrive at solutions that benefit you both.

When one partner has stated his or her needs, concerns, or requests, be grateful for the sharing. Say thank you, reflect back, and switch roles. The other partner then has a chance to talk about his/her concerns regarding the particular issue and ask for what he/she desires. The listener can write down what is heard without reacting or judging, and reflect back. The speaker can then add, clarify, or approve what was said.

Be encouraging. Avoid disagreeing or criticizing what your partner said. Put aside any anger or frustration and stop yourself from preparing your defense. Remember that his or her words are merely opinions that you may or may not agree with. You will eventually get a chance to express yourself. Watch your body language and facial expressions. A frown or scowl will cause your partner to shut down or get angry. Remind yourself to be an active listener and stay present.

You may ask clarifying questions such as:

- Help me understand why you feel that way.

- Can you tell me more about that?

- How do you feel now?

- How does this remind you of something that has happened in the past?

- What you would like?

At times, each person may take longer to express concerns. One partner may respond quickly, and the other will need to think for a while before answering. If you are connecting at a deep level, you may be able to see how your previous experiences have impacted the present problem. For example, if Jordan felt that he was nagged by his mother, he might connect the dots and recognize that he transferred his feeling of being controlled onto his wife, even when she wasn't nagging.

When Kathy and Jordan took turns speaking, they examined their concerns. Jordan shared his anxiety about paying the bills, the expense of remodeling the kitchen, and the fear of not having money for the children's education.

With coaching, Kathy listened attentively and mirrored back that Jordan was exhausted from working overtime for the sake of his family, and that he felt anxious about money. She asked him to tell her more about feeling overwhelmed. He revealed how frightening it was as a child when his parents struggled financially to raise five children.

6. Ask and answer open-ended questions about how to resolve the issue.

After both parties have had their concerns reflected back, each person will ask open-ended questions about possible solutions, such as:

- What are you needing or wanting from me?

- What would work for you?

- How can we meet each other's needs?

- What are some solutions that meet our concerns?

Reflect back your partner's answers to make sure you understood. If you wrote them down, you could read them back. Courteously, remind one another that there are no judgments or put-downs. After you practice effective listening and clarifying, you can move into the next step.

7. Brainstorm various alternatives.

Do not start negotiating solutions yet. When you and your partner listen without criticizing or judging during the brainstorming, creative solutions become possible. Your partner's personality is not the problem. The situation or the behavior is the challenge that needs to be seen in a new way. Separating your lover's character from the behavior that is offensive allows you to explore new approaches to create better outcomes.

Instead of Jordan telling Kathy that she's a nag, he can tell her that when she continually remarks about not enough time together, he feels pressured and uncomfortable. He can also acknowledge that he appreciates her love. Instead of Kathy characterizing Jordan as a selfish workaholic, she can let him know that she feels abandoned and lonely when he is gone all week. She can appreciate how hard he works to support the family.

As you brainstorm possible solutions, respond as a problem solver instead of a problem maker. After you have actively clarified suggestions for meeting each other's needs, list all possible solutions. Make sure the suggestions are what you *do* want, not what you don't want. Collaborate in narrowing down possible options that are mutually acceptable. This process of working together to invent options creates a feeling of teamwork and connection.

In the example, Kathy and Jordan brainstormed some alternatives:

> Jordan suggested that he could try to get a new job closer to home. Until that happened, he would ask his boss if he could work from home part-time and reduce overtime. To do that, he suggested creating a budget to spend less money. He would take the kids to sports practice, even if it meant spending more time working evenings to catch up. He encouraged Kathy to get a babysitter on two Saturday nights a month for date nights.

> Kathy suggested that she could get a part-time job or start a career from home since the kids were in school during the day. That way, Jordan wouldn't have to work such long hours. The family would have more funds available for a vacation, and they wouldn't have to skimp on the budget. To deal with home care, she could get a cleaning service every other week, or have

the kids contribute with chores around the house. She offered to take the kids to grandma's house every couple of months for the weekend, so that she and Jordan could be alone for more romantic moments.

8. Clarify options and jointly consider a proposal.

Once you have jointly made a list of possible solutions for the issues at hand, consider the options. Evaluate each of the suggestions and clarify which ones are most workable, and how you could implement them. During this selection stage, avoid criticizing or blaming. You can discuss the pros and cons of each suggestion and circle those that are most comfortable for you. Each of you will have the opportunity to express concerns. Be clear about what is acceptable and unacceptable and why. Again, if you become angry, stay calm or take a break. Slowly explain your reasoning without attacking.

Here's how Jordan and Kathy responded to their list:

Jordan proposed that he would look for a job closer to home. Until then, he would either work longer hours four days a week and come home early on Fridays, or if his boss agreed, he would work from home part of the time. On those days, he would take the kids to practice. He agreed with the idea of getting a babysitter and taking the kids to their grandparents, so he and Kathy could spend time alone. However, he was concerned about using a cleaning service.

Kathy proposed that she restart her career and work part-time to earn money for the family. If she was able to get a job, she would hire a cleaning service once a week. She would also give the kids an allowance for cleaning their rooms and doing their laundry.

9. Finalize your agreement.

To help you clarify your expectations and establish accountability, write an agreement (see sample below). Include who will do what and when, with a specific timeline for actions with a reassessment of how it went. Writing your agreement provides clarity, commitment, and follow-through. It also reminds the parties of their part in the process. If need be, the agreement can always be amended.

Once you and your partner are comfortable with a proposal, commit to trying the agreement for a couple of weeks. Follow up with a meeting in two weeks to assess and share feedback about what works and what doesn't. Remember, problems are not caused by character flaws; they are the result of misunderstanding, miscommunication, misperceptions, or changed circumstances

The couple's agreement looked like this:

Jordan And Kathy's Working Agreement

We commit to spend more time together and with the children. Each of us agrees to the following:

1. Jordan will talk with his boss next week to present a plan for him to work at home two days a week. If that is not workable, Jordan will go in at 6:00 a.m. and leave at 2:00 p.m. at least two days a week. If he is able to work from home or come home early, he will take the kids to sports practice on those two days.

2. Kathy will get a babysitter on the first and third Saturday night each month. She and Jordan will alternate planning the date night. Kathy will call her mom to see if she will agree to come to the family home quarterly for the weekend, beginning next month and watch the kids so that Kathy and Jordan can have a romantic getaway.

3. Kathy will explore a part-time job. If she is able to start working, she will research a cleaning service for twice a month. She will create a proposed budget by no later than the first of the month.

4. Kathy and Jordan will jointly prepare a list of chores with the kids, indicating what each child will do in the home and how much allowance they will receive.

5. We agree to complete the tasks by next Saturday night when we meet at seven o'clock.

Date: _____

Kathy: _____

Jordan: _____

To be successful at solutioneering, you may not get everything you want, but you will get your most important needs met when you willingly work together to meet each other's concerns. The old adage, "Two heads are better than one," indicates that collaboration helps you be more creative in finding solutions.

Both of you will have unique perspectives, so calmly and politely offer your views and consider options that meet your partner's concerns. A take it or leave it attitude doesn't achieve solutions. Instead, it escalates hostility. Your willingness to accept your loved one's right to see the world differently creates an atmosphere of mutual respect. This results in a peaceful and intimate relationship. Collaboration and honesty build bridges of connection.

10. Meet again and follow up to see if you need to adjust the agreement, and celebrate that you turned conflict into harmony and intimacy.

After you tried out an agreement, you may need to adjust it, especially if the circumstances changed. You don't have to be rigid about sticking to the letter of the agreement if you find a better solution. If you need a change in the agreement, set up an appointment and discuss it. Good communication and follow-through establish trust, an essential ingredient to a successful relationship.

Reaching agreement on any issue fosters greater intimacy. Some agreements may come easily and quickly; others may require several meetings over a period of time. You may need to gather additional information, and/or you may need time to let your emotions simmer so that you can focus on positively moving forward.

In the next chapter, we will focus on the Hard Love strategy to deal with more difficult issues and high-conflict emotions that cause lovers to become hostile. Some say the closest thing to love is hate. When individuals are angry, and there is persistent antagonism, solutioneering needs to be combined with Hard Love.

FIGHTING FOR LOVE EXERCISES:

Consider a recurring dispute between you and your partner, such as an issue regarding money, sex, childcare, chores, etc. Name the issue that seems to be a persistent challenge between you and your loved one. How do you approach that problem?

Using solutioneering, move through the following steps to resolve the issue. Eliminate blame or accusations from your approach as you try the following:

1. When you have identified a challenge, plan a time and day to meet. Jot down how you want to approach the situation ahead of time, remembering to see it as an issue to be resolved, not an opportunity to find fault with your partner.

2. Start your discussion with positive loving statements expressing gratitude for things your partner has recently done.

3. Calmly bring up a concern that you have without blaming or criticizing.

4. Actively listen and reflect back what you heard.

5. Take turns stating your needs and concerns.

6. Ask and answer open-ended questions about how you may resolve the issue.

7. Brainstorm various alternatives.

8. Clarify options and jointly consider proposals.

9. Finalize an agreement with a written summary of what each has agreed to do.

10. Meet again and follow up to see if you need to adjust the agreement, and celebrate that you turned conflict into harmony and intimacy.

"Whenever you're mad at me, visit my
web page. I have a searchable database
of apologies and excuses for every occasion!"

CHAPTER 11

Transform Hostility with Hard Love

If you are patient in one moment of anger, you will escape one hundred days of sorrow.

— Chinese Proverb

Arlene and Elliot were married fifteen years. When Elliot became angry, he shouted at his wife. Fearing her husband's outbursts, Arlene kept her feelings inside. She expressed her hostility through passive-aggressiveness behavior, such as *accidentally* burning his meals. Eventually, Arlene grew sick and tired of Elliot's raging outbursts. She wanted out. She and her husband sought mediation. There, Arlene learned that she had the power to change herself by using the Hard Love strategy.

In the last chapter, we provided you with steps to use interest-based negotiation skills to deflect conflict and get what you need. But if one or both of you have a high-conflict personality, meaning a short fuse, you need the "Hard Love" strategy. It not only deflects conflict, but it provides a process to reverse bitterness and transform your fighting into love.

Please note: this chapter is not about domestic violence. If you are the subject of physical abuse, you need to remove yourself from the situation and go to a safe place, contact law enforcement, and seek individual counseling. Your and your children's safety is the primary concern.

The following strategies address escalating anger, accusations, and verbal mistreatment. Those behaviors demolish love.

If your partner shouts offensive accusations, blames you, or ignores your concerns, do you have a right to be upset? Of course. Your anger is a natural emotion, somewhat like a fire alarm is meant to protect you from danger. Even the most agreeable couple will have, at times, legitimate feelings of resentment. Why? Because when expectations and hopes about the relationship seem to be dissolving, there will be disappointment and pain. Animosity can grow out of feelings of rejection and perceived intentional wrongs. Unfortunately, the legitimate suffering that you experience in a hostile relationship can deteriorate into an acrimonious marriage, an exhausting breakup, or an expensive courtroom divorce battle. Anger that comes out destructively tears the bonds of loving relationships.

There's a saying that irritation unexpressed leads to anger. Anger unexpressed leads to rage, and rage unexpressed leads to prison. The amygdala is the area of our emotional brain that processes emotions and reacts to fear and pleasure. When we feel threatened and become hostile from intense anger, we may experience emotional hijacking. Our rational mind becomes overwhelmed by emotions. In that state, we may react by fighting, fleeing, or freezing. These reactions are automatic and are a result of internal distress. This makes it more likely for us to resort to criticism and contempt or become pessimistic about our relationship.

Without an outlet for the healthy expression of unresolved hurt and unmet needs, we will either send the suppressed anger underground or meet hostility with aggression. Both actions will fuel the flames of resentment and create a toxic relationship. When we "lose it," our primitive mind will blurt out words we will regret. As Elizabeth Kenny, a nurse who courageously and successfully fought polio and the medical community, once said, "He who angers you conquers you."

If we allow anger to rule our lives, it becomes our master. However, it becomes our friend when we recognize that something in our life needs to change or heal. Sometimes we may be furious at our partner, but the problem may be an unresolved issue that we had with a parent or former lover. It may be anger at something we did or didn't do, or someone else. It's sometimes too easy to take out our frustrations on loved ones who are there to support us. Negative emotions from the past or present often sneak into our intimate relationships.

We want to handle our emotions effectively, lest they impair our reasoning and decision-making. Therefore, it's crucial that we retain our power and dignity by managing our anger. When we are upset, we can use tools to manage intense emotions and steer through them toward a positive outcome.

The goal of this chapter is to help you *consciously* respond, not instinctively overreact. Below is a proven strategy that you can use any time your loved one, or anyone else for that matter, heatedly attacks your ideas, actions, or beliefs. Mari coined the acronym HARD LOVE for this eight-step strategy to transform conflict to intimacy.

HARD LOVE

H = HALT

If your partner says anything that offends you, stop yourself from reacting by mentally telling yourself, "Halt!" Don't say anything until you can recover from the attack. If you hear something nasty like, "You bitch," or, "You're just like your father," don't allow the knee-jerk reaction to take hold of you. Avoid expressing negative emotions. Instead, be aware of any tension in your body such as tight shoulders, a knot in your stomach, or an ache in your head. Now pay attention to your breathing. Slow it down. Repeat this until you feel calmer. Focus on your breath, not your anger.

A = ANGER CONTROL

Anger and frustration get stored in your physical body. It is nature's way of protecting you from danger. When you are upset, scan your body. Become aware of where the negative sensations are held. You can decipher how you react to hostility by doing the following: Close your eyes and remember something your partner said that made you feel furious. For example, being told that you are selfish or narcissistic. As you recall the statement, direct your mind to your physical senses. What do you feel in the throes of anger? Identify your own physical reaction to verbal battle. Get out of your head and into your body. Some typical reactions to hostility are dryness in the throat, stiffness in the neck, a stabbing knife in the solar plexus, tightness in the chest or shoulders, or a burning feeling in one's face.

Once you recognize your body's auto-reply to verbal attack, you'll gain the insight to override its power over you. Your body's negative physical reaction often occurs in the same area every time you feel fury. By quickly turning your attention to the physical reaction, you become aware of what is happening in your body. Recognition allows your logical brain to stop the uncontrolled reaction. You can then make a conscious decision to soothe your emotions. From a calm place, you will more effectively manage the anger.

R = REVERSE NEGATIVE REACTION

Once you give the stressful part of your body attention, breathe into it and relax without fighting the feeling. Continued breathing into that area reverses the overpowering response to retaliate. When you see yourself as an observer of your body's reaction, you lean into the feeling and gently let it calm you. That allows you to get centered and adopt a more logical approach.

You can deliberately change your body's reaction by creating a thought that reverses the sensations. For example, if you feel a knife in your solar plexus when accused or offended, imagine in your mind's eye that you are gently removing the weapon with no ill effect.

If your throat becomes dry, envision yourself drinking refreshing water. To reverse a rush of heat to your face, send yourself a cool breeze. See a powerful and soothing reversal for any uncomfortable feeling that manifests when your body reacts to hostile feelings. Once you know what image works for you, you can instantly remedy a triggered reaction whenever you feel increasingly angry. This practice can become a habit to draw upon when you need to manage your emotions.

Whenever you wish to deflect anger, remember to mindfully focus your breathing into the tense areas of your body and picture yourself instantly serene. If you have difficulty releasing the stress, consciously tighten the muscles around the tense area, then release and let go. This will help you rebalance your body and emotions. With practice, your gentle reversal of your auto-reaction to conflict will take only a few seconds. Thus far, you have still not uttered a word back to the attacker.

Before you speak, regain your mental composure, so you will be in control of your emotions. This will enable you to resolve an issue with your partner in a positive manner.

D = DISENGAGE

When you have detached from the anger physically, you are ready to disengage mentally from negativity. Focus on the issue itself, not your partner's character. Avoid name-calling. If you were called selfish, look behind the comment and the behavior. Consider that he/she was angry about a need that was not met.

Your partner's hurtful words are just perceptions and not facts. In truth, lashing out tells you there is something deeper going on that has not been resolved. Don't allow yourself to buy into offensive statements as a threat to your character. Your significant other's outbursts are just thoughts, not your reality. You don't have to be defensive or convince him/her otherwise. By releasing any need to prove you are right, you de-escalate the conflict. You know your truth. When you detach yourself from the tornado of hostility, the storm will subside. If you don't engage, there is no war. However, that doesn't mean that you ignore the issue that angered you.

Staying calm is not a sign of defeat or that you agree. It just stops the battle. If your partner cannot engage you in a battle, he/she can't win control over you. If you are like most people, you probably don't want to feel manipulated or dominated. In the midst of heated arguments, your job is to manage your own emotions. Not an easy task. If your significant other has succumbed to his/her own anger, and you don't react in kind, you retain your dignity. You are in charge of your feelings and need not to be sucked into an unproductive clash.

L = LISTEN EFFECTIVELY

In steps one through four, you have detached physically and mentally and disengaged from your lover's argument. The next step is to listen to every word without resistance. This doesn't mean you agree. Don't prepare your response while your partner speaks. Be present and listen. Demonstrate a willingness to understand with respect. Noncontentious, nondefensive listening deflects hostility and gives you powerful information to resolve the real issues.

For example, if you were told, "You're selfish and narcissistic," it may be tough to hear. Instead of reacting negatively, listen to your partner's emotions behind the words and watch his/her body language from an observer's viewpoint. Be in the now, actively listen, and be ready to show that you heard your partner.

O = OPENLY MIRROR

This step takes you back to the solutioneering process. However, it will be different here because the emotions are far more intense. Although you probably won't feel respected hearing caustic remarks, let them go. Remember, the comments are your partner's words. They represent anger or frustration and are not the truth about you. His/her outbursts are coming from the reactive part of the brain that is not logical.

Take the high road by showing you actually listened to your partner respectfully. Listening is a form of loving. Restate calmly and sincerely, in a neutral tone, the essence of what your partner said. For example, you could reframe "selfish" by saying, "I heard that you say that I am not giving to you." You may follow up with, "Do I understand you correctly?"

Your partner may respond with a yes or no and clarify further. Every time your loved one clarifies, reflect back what you heard. Ask if you heard correctly what was said.

Here are a few more examples of reframing negative statements:

Mary: *You stole all our money!*

Rick: *You're upset with me because you think I spend too much money and the bank account is low.*

Sam: *You are a liar!*

Sue: *So you think I'm not being honest with you.*

Mirroring and reframing your partner's hostile words does not mean you have agreed with what they said. You are only demonstrating your understanding of what you heard. You give the gift of love by hearing your loved one's perceptions and feelings without being defensive or offensive. When you listen attentively, you model how you wish to be heard. This will encourage your partner to reciprocate.

V = VOICE OPEN-ENDED QUESTIONS

In the steps above, you have mindfully composed yourself and have shown that you heard your partner by mirroring and understanding their concerns. You now follow up a mirrored statement with open-ended questions or engaging statements.

- "Please tell me why you feel that way."

- "Help me understand what you mean."

- "What makes you think that way?"

Information-gathering questions or statements elicit revealing responses. In a curious or neutral tone, pose clarifying questions like:

- What do you mean?

- How will that work?

- When can you do that?

- Tell me more about your concerns.

- How can we both get our needs met?

These types of open-ended questions or statements give your partner a chance to move out of his/her primitive, emotionally reactive brain and regain composure. He or she is then more likely to respond from the frontal lobes of the brain and be more calm and logical.

After your partner answers your clarifying questions, mirror the responses again. Keep reflecting back to show you understand the underlying feelings and needs. You may add, "That's helpful to understand. Tell me more about that." Listening actively shows your partner that you value what he/she is saying. It is one of the most important tools to resolving conflict.

E = EMBRACE SOLUTIONS

This step shifts you and your partner into the brainstorming stage of proposing various options that resolve the current issue. Both of you need to share ways to deflect the hostility now and in the future. If you have difficulty moving toward solutions, you may need to practice some of the forgiveness exercises outlined in Chapter 8.

As you move forward with any brainstorming, make a list of what you could both do differently during times of intense conflict. Then you can jointly analyze the alternatives. Ask each other questions that solicit proposals for healing the conflict:

- What would you like me to do?

- What do you suggest?

- How can we handle this in the future?

- What are some things we can do now?

- What are your thoughts about how we can both feel satisfied?

- What are your underlying needs and concerns?

- What do you believe would be fair under the circumstances?

After you have heard your partner's suggestions, share your feelings and concerns in a non-accusatory manner. Use "I" Messages, such as "If we agree to have a brief time out when tempers flare, I will feel more comfortable to come back and focus on problem solving."

If you blame your partner while discussing issues, he/she will probably not want to brainstorm solutions. Blame begets blame and accusations call for cross-accusations. Be careful of an "I" statement that points the "you" finger at your partner, such as, "I feel you are wrong." That kind of statement escalates conflict.

In the example of a partner accusing the other of being selfish and narcissistic, this is one way to handle the conversation:

Beverly: *You're selfish and narcissistic.*

Tom: (He first breathes into his chest to release tightness and get centered.) *I heard you say that you think I am not generous. Is that what you mean?*

Beverly: *You can be generous with gifts, but when I need help with the kids, you just sit on the couch and watch sports. You think only of yourself.*

Tom: *I appreciate you recognizing that I can be generous. You want more help with the children, right?*

Beverly: *Absolutely!*

Tom: *Let's work out something together so the kids' needs are met and we're both happy.*

To fight for love fairly, consider making an agreement that neither blames nor accuses the other. If there is a breach of the agreement, gently notify your partner of the rift and arrange a time to have a conversation. Set boundaries about how you will speak to each other in heated discussions.

Sometimes old patterns of arguing are so ingrained that we will easily fall back into judging and accusatory behaviors. However, we can retrain ourselves to create new habits. This requires a commitment to relate differently. No matter how aggressive or unkind our partner may get, we can avoid reacting. Again, easier said than done. But if we calmly pause before responding, concentrate on breathing slowly, listen without engaging in hostility, and respond in a softer tone of voice, we will shift the emotional climate to a more peaceful interchange. We may have to repeat those steps during a discussion to transform the energy. As long as we remain conscious of how we are feeling in our body, we can manage the stressful physical responses and avoid losing control, which escalates the conflict.

If you find that you or your partner still cannot calm down, remove yourself with dignity *before* you get hooked into more frustration. If you can't control or manage your own emotions, take a break. If you're speaking on the phone, calmly end the conversation. This allows you both to reconvene without groveling. If you or your partner has been drinking alcohol or taken drugs, or are sick, exhausted or hungry, make time to talk later, especially when there is a hot issue.

Sometimes, exercising alone or walking together will release the physical tension, thereby creating a better climate for a conversation. At other times, a short break to meditate or pray resets the balance. Alternately, a public venue can offer a place where there are more constraints on overreacting.

If you're tempted to sweep concerns under the rug for fear of a blowout, wait until you are ready to talk, but don't wait too long or resentment will build. Make sure both of you choose a mutually convenient time to meet. If you avoid discussions about painful feelings, tension will come out insidiously and make the situation much worse.

There may be times when counseling will help you and your partner sort through difficult problems. You can explore and clarify the origin of your issues, recognize the trigger points, and discover alternate ways of handling them. Coaching from an experienced counselor can help you see patterns that foster conflict and walk you through the steps to resolve recurring issues. At the same time, you and your loved one can be guided on the path toward greater intimacy.

Is It Time to Move On?

If you and your partner have tried counseling, worked on your relationship, or your partner has taken on another lover, you may need to let go of that bond and work on healing yourself. Living in a toxic or nonsupportive situation can be extremely draining. If the two of you no longer share common values and goals and spend most of your time battling one another, or your partner refuses to get help, recognize that you did the best you could with the knowledge you had. You both traveled together for a while and probably had some wonderful times. You can still be grateful for the love and the learning that you received as you releasing the bond.

Your recovery and renewal may be painful, but it will lead to the gift of growth and transformation. Any time you experience a loss, you are called to rediscover who you are, what you want, and what you need. It may be difficult to endure a breakup while grieving, but you can still be gentle and nurturing toward yourself. As one door closes, another one opens. Give yourself time to grieve the loss, forgive the past, and value each other as individuals. Even if you felt betrayed, you must move on. Mutual respect is especially important if you have children together. They still need parents who collaborate together and convey the message that they are loved.

When a couple dissolves a relationship, they can choose not to act out their anger and frustration in a toxic manner. If they are married, they may agree not to further hurt themselves and their families in a protracted and costly stressful court battle. Instead, they can opt for a private, collaborative divorce mediation to help them peacefully resolve the legal issues of property, finances, and child custody. Although ending any love relationship involves a grieving process, there is less agony and more growth when the parties move through a cooperative process, especially if children are involved. Mutual respect and collaboration is essential to raise healthy children.

If you divorce, consider using a qualified attorney-mediator who has the skills to help you decrease the hostility and positively resolve the legal issues. An experienced professional will help you divide the assets and debts and protect you and your children from further pain. Divorce is highly emotional. Resolving difficult issues in a public forum before a judge who doesn't know you or have sufficient time to properly hear you out will only frustrate you further and dissipate your marital funds.

Litigation escalates conflict by encouraging partners to accuse one another about the past so the judge can rule against one or both. With mediation, you and your spouse are empowered to make your own decisions within the realm of the law about your future without an expensive, stressful, court contest. Mediation encourages you to focus on the present, forgive each other, and positively move on with your lives.

No matter the outcome of your relationship, whether you evolve together as a team and expand your love, or separate to grow as individuals, you are capable of transforming conflict. As you improve yourself, your relationships will change.

You fight for love by restoring peace in your life and accepting yourself. In the next chapter, we will discuss how to heal conflicts from the inside out. Doing so will help you be more loving to yourself and your partner.

FIGHTING FOR LOVE EXERCISES:

Consider a situation with your significant other that made you extremely angry.

1. How did you deal with your own hostility?

2. Was your reaction to fight, freeze, or flee?

3. How did your partner respond to you?

4. How do you hold anger in your body?

5. When angry, what thoughts do you have?

6. What can you do in the future to manage your anger so it doesn't master you?

"I do so share my deepest emotions with you!
Hungry and tired are my deepest emotions."

CHAPTER 12

Heal from the Inside Out

---

*First, all relationships are with yourself —
and sometimes they involve other people.
Second, the most important relationship in
your life — the one you have, like it or not,
until the day you die — is with yourself.*

— Peter McWilliams

*Happiness cannot come from
without. It must come from within.*

— Helen Keller

Rodney constantly complained that Alison controlled his life. She told him what to wear, how to comb his hair, how to manage customers, and how to treat their grown kids. He would yell at Alison to stop micromanaging his life. Even though she acknowledged that she was a control freak, she said that she acted that way out of love for him. When the arguments escalated, Rodney would explode, causing Alison to feel out of control. Clearly, Rodney and Alison needed to understand their own part in the recurring battles and take steps to heal from the inside out.

We are each responsible for our own thoughts, emotions, and actions. However, our immediate impulse is to look outside ourselves for the cause of pain. If we blame others, or if we feel guilty, we choose to be a victim. Alternately, we can take responsibility for our part in what has happened in the relationship and look within to recognize our inner discord. We can then shine the light on our thoughts, feelings, and actions. Doing so helps us recognize what no longer serves us.

We will probably discover unhealed wounds from the past. They can become a motivating force for change. If we step on a thorn, we can either wait for someone else to remove it or extract it ourselves. We don't have to walk around in pain and expect our partner to remove it. We can learn from the conflict, heal from the pain, and take steps to change.

M. Scott Peck wrote, "The truth is that our finest moments are most likely to occur when we are feeling deeply uncomfortable, unhappy, or unfulfilled. For it is only in such moments, propelled by our discomfort, that we are likely to step out of our ruts and start searching for different ways or truer answers." Discomfort provokes us to transform our lives. Most of us can recall painful situations that have helped us develop character and even achieve great triumphs.

All conflict in our lives is really an inside job. If you are ending a relationship, you need time to grieve and nurture yourself. In times of despair, you may not realize that you have within you a remarkable ability to heal.

You can reach out and receive caring from friends, family, counselors, spiritual advisors, even pets. By allowing yourself to grieve, you will arise again, like the phoenix rising from the ashes. If you do feel overwhelmed and unable to see a bright future, by all means, see a counselor. He or she will shine the light on your life and help you through the process.

As you learn new tools to resolve inner conflict and effectively express your needs and desires, you will notice positive changes occurring in your life. The greatest improvements come from being the change you wish to see in others.

Mary and her husband were in the interior design and building business for fifteen years. Although she was a talented designer, she had wanted to be a counselor ever since she was a teen. As a result of her divorce, she was no longer part of the family business. The breakup devastated her but altered her perspective. She decided to move on with her life and take the opportunity to go back to school. This turned her life around. She became a successful family therapist and developed a loving relationship with herself and, eventually, a new partner.

The following process provides more steps that you can take to become your own supportive counselor. You can let go of your distress and heal yourself from the inside out.

1. Observe your internal conflict.

Whenever you experience inner turmoil, the first step to self-healing is to observe yourself physically, emotionally, and mentally in a nonjudgmental manner. Start by being mindful of your physical sensations. Act as an observer and notice them.

If you are anxious or tense, scan your body and observe how you are feeling in your muscles and joints. You may be clenching your jaw or slouching your shoulders. You may be frowning or furrowing your brow. Your stomach may be tight or your heart may be racing. As you pay attention to the discomfort, become more present to your body. Breathe deeply and slowly into those areas where you hold the pain. Imagine a loving energy filling any area of discomfort. Relax into that loving energy.

Once you connect with your body, bring your awareness to your emotions. There are no right or wrong feelings, for they are merely messengers to help you pay attention. Give yourself permission to let the emotions surface. If you are angry, sad, fearful, ashamed, or guilty, just breathe into them. Be the observer of what you are feeling. As you pay attention to them, allow them to dissolve and dissipate.

After you notice your physical sensations and emotions, become conscious of your thoughts. It's easy to get lost in negative thoughts and to believe that what you think is reality. Just because you have thoughts does not mean they are true. Become aware of what is happening in your mind. You, like most of us, go through our day on autopilot, reacting out of habit. Have you ever started the day, getting ready for work, and not remembered taking a shower, brushing your teeth, or getting dressed? Have you ever driven to work and not recalled the details of the trip? That's living on remote control. You have the ability to become aware of your thoughts and to control them.

To be more aware of how you are thinking, ask your-self the following questions:

- What am I telling myself?

- Am I stuck in thoughts about my partner, whether he or she has wronged me, or whether I have hurt him or her?

- What am I feeling now and why?

- How do I know what I am thinking is true?

- What do I need to feel better?

- How can I express myself in a way that is not defensive or blaming?

- What positive thoughts can I choose about myself and the situation right now?

Notice your answers. What are you telling yourself? If you felt hurt by something your partner said or did, you might be replaying that scenario in your mind. You could perceive yourself as a victim, righteously indignant, or you could feel guilty about being a bully.

When we are in emotional pain, we have a tendency to repeat negative thoughts, as if replaying an old movie. "If I hadn't said that, she wouldn't have left," or "If only I had been more sexual, he would not have had the affair." The mind gets trapped in a self-perpetuating loop. Focused attention helps us recognize what we are thinking so we can stop repeating the movie. As we begin to notice repetitive patterns, we can take charge and make empowering decisions such as:

I did the best I could at the time.

I didn't understand what she wanted, but now I know how to communicate better.

I learned from this situation and will do things differently in the future.

Here are more questions to help you understand your thinking:

- When you don't feel heard or are upset that your needs are not met in the relationship, what do you do?

- Are you able to trust your partner?

- What makes you feel loved or unloved in relationships?

- Do you feel victimized, disrespected, or powerless? If so, what does that remind you of in the past?

- Do you have a need to be in control? If you feel out of control, what does that remind you of in the past?

Your patterns will emerge as you shine the light of awareness on those inward thoughts and beliefs. When you stop and observe what's going on with your body, emotions, and mind, you become conscious of the impact of inner conflict on your life. You can choose to make healthy changes and move toward acceptance.

2. Accept yourself.

Accepting yourself exactly the way you are right now offsets any tendency to negatively judge yourself. This doesn't mean you are perfect, or that there is no need to change certain behaviors and beliefs. When you are hurting or have lost a relationship, it's natural to feel sad. You may have a tendency to feel guilty, inadequate, or unlovable. These thoughts are not reality; they are just your reactive perceptions to a situation. Accept, in a loving manner, where you are. Consider that you are like the caterpillar in a cocoon, growing within and trans-forming, getting ready to emerge as a butterfly.

Self-acceptance establishes a gentle connection between you as the observer and that which you are observing, as if you are in a helicopter watching yourself. This is an important step to remove yourself from the chaos of negative thoughts and establish a new direction. When you acknowledge your situation, you move forward. The Buddha said, "All suffering comes from not accepting what is." As you accept that you did the best you could, with the understanding and information that you had at the time, you can move forward and love yourself.

Roger was a successful electrical engineer with a beautiful wife, Rebecca. They had four adorable children. One day, he came home early while the kids were at school and found his wife in bed with her personal trainer. Though he became outraged about the affair, Roger didn't want to end the marriage. Rebecca told him that she hoped to remain married but was not prepared to give up her lover. Roger wanted so much to keep his family together that he initially agreed to the arrangement. However, over time, he became very despondent and resentful, believing he was an incompetent husband. He finally accepted the reality of the situation and knew he had to take better care of himself and the children. He could no longer accept the ongoing affair and decided to dissolve the marriage. This prompted him to join a men's support group who helped him to recognize and talk about his feelings. Roger realized that traveling for work away from home played a part in the lack of intimacy with his wife. This started him on his own journey of self-discovery. He became committed to changing himself. That included negotiating boundaries and communicating more honestly with his wife in mediation. Roger's inner healing had a profound effect on the marriage. His transformation reignited the sparks in the relationship.

Recognition of what is happening brings you a sense of relief, for it cuts through denial. You become aware that you have courageously revealed your current state of being, and you gently move to a deeper place of introspection. If, for example, you observe yourself moving into self-blame, you can acknowledge it, rather than berate yourself. That acknowledgment exposes your need to forgive yourself. From acceptance, you move to forgiveness where you free yourself from the anguish of the past.

3. Practice forgiveness—the key to freedom.

In Chapter 8, we talked about forgiveness and the three R's. We recognize the distress, release the pain, and resolve the issues by letting go of the resentment that binds us to the past. Practicing the three R's sounds simple but, in reality, it takes time and effort to implement because our ego wants to be right. If we self-righteously point out how we were wronged, we may momentarily feel vindicated, believing we are the better person. However, that position leaves us with resentment and makes us a victim. If we hold grudges or engage in the win/lose game in love, we are the losers.

As we forgive our partner for something that was said or done, we let go of critical thoughts and emotions that would otherwise fester. Forgiveness sets us free from feelings that eat us up inside. The act of forgiveness also allows us to accept an apology and hold our loved one accountable to change and grow from the conflictual situation. Forgiveness is a gift we give to ourselves for our own peace of mind. Even if we end the relationship, forgiveness helps us close the door to negativity so that a new door of happiness can be opened.

To forgive ourselves for something we said or did is liberating. It means giving up the attack in our mind for not acting as we think we should. Forgiveness offers a remedy and a countermeasure to sooth our mind and release judgments, preconceptions, resentments, and guilt. It is the practice of giving up the destructive negative emotions that enables us to receive the gift of growth. Forgiveness also asks us to make amends to the ones we have hurt.

Forgiveness, like the practice of observation or acceptance, creates a shift in consciousness. Resentment and revenge tear down relationships, while forgiveness builds connections and heals relationships with ourselves and others. This leads to self-love.

4. Love yourself.

The greatest improvement you can make is to create a more loving relationship with yourself. There is often a stigma to loving ourselves, which has been equated with being conceited, boastful, arrogant, and selfish. If you feel embarrassed saying, "I love myself," consider that self-love is an acceptance of who you are. You have come into existence to evolve and give and receive love. As you become more aware of the true essence of love and honor and nurture it, you will give more love to others. They, in turn, will respond to you in a more loving manner.

Ask yourself these questions:

- How do I feel when I love myself?

- If I love myself, how do I act in the world?

- What can I do to show more self-love?

5. Clarify what you desire in your love life.

You have observed and accepted your sensations, feelings, and thoughts and practiced forgiveness and self-love. Now consider these questions:

- How do I want to feel now?

- What do I need or desire now?

- How do I want to change or grow?

When feeling disconnected from your loved one, whether during an argument or a breakup, you may intermittently feel a host of emotions, such as rage, sadness, hurt, frustration, or guilt. However, you can ask yourself, "What is my inner conflict about? What are we really fighting about? What's in our highest good?" These questions help you clarify your feelings and understand what is most important. Beneath conflict and inner turmoil, there is often a hurt inner child who needs understanding and love.

The very act of asking the above questions establishes an intention to focus on the present moment. When you are embroiled in negative emotions, you may have difficulty locating your inner desires. If you feel blocked, center yourself with deep breathing and connect with your body and emotions. Then tell yourself, "I release this negativity. I now focus on seeing a solution to this problem. I am open and receptive to an answer that works for both of us."

Clarifying, understanding, and managing your emotions and what you want in life help you heal from the inside out. You may desire more understanding, appreciation, compassion, or intimacy. If you are not clear what you want, your partner will not know what you need, and you will have difficulty achieving a satisfying relationship. As you use self-reflection and inquiry, you welcome awareness, appreciation, genuine love, and self-healing.

6. Imagine harmony and success in your relationship.

Once you identify what you desire and how you want to relate in a loving relationship, imagine how that would feel and look when your desires are satisfied. What sensations would you experience in your body? Visualize yourself in a loving partnership. Consider how easily and effortlessly you would communicate and listen to each other. Envision increased intimacy as you share feelings and resolve differences.

Visualization, or active imagination, is a powerful tool that successful people use to create an image in their mind. For example, elite athletes visualize peak performances to enhance their game. Phil Jackson, who successfully coached the Chicago Bulls to six championships and then the Los Angeles Lakers to five championships, described his use of meditation and visualization in *Sacred Hoops*. He wrote, "Visualization is the bridge I use to link the grand vision of the team I conjure up every summer to the evolving reality on the court. That vision becomes a working sketch that I adjust, refine, and sometimes scrap altogether as the season develops."

A number of famous people attribute visualization as a key to their success. These include: Oprah Winfrey; Bill Gates; Jim Carrey; and Rhonda Byrne who wrote the bestselling book, *The Secret*.

Actually, you practice visualization all the time. When you plan a vacation, you create pictures in your mind of your travels, the activities you will be doing, and the fun you will be having. You also do this when you are worried about any future activity. You actually create a mental movie with your thoughts when you plan your day.

Shakti Gawain wrote *Creative Visualization* in which she explained how our thoughts create our reality. If we believe our relationship is a loving one, we picture that in our mind's eye and act out of love. Our mental picture creates the thoughts, action, and momentum that lead us to fulfill the vision.

You can utilize the principles of visualization to program your mind with powerful affirmative mental states that manifest what you desire. If you actively see yourself holding hands, hugging, and kissing your partner, and he or she smiles at you in a loving way, you, in effect, embed those images in your mind. Over time, you start to act more loving and attract those desired responses in your loved one as well.

You have the ability to direct your thoughts to clarify your feelings, needs, and plan of action. As you give yourself the gift of acceptance, forgiveness, understanding, nurturing, and love, you heal from the inside out. You are now ready to create the love you want in your relationship.

7. Act in a way that satisfies your relationship desires.

To manifest the picture and loving emotional state you create through active imagination, ask yourself, "What can I do right now on my own to satisfy my needs and desires?" Take actions that support positive outcomes and empower you to shift from a negative state into one that is uplifting. If you need to release anger, frustration, or unhappiness, consider activities that allow you to express that energy, such as vigorous exercise.

Make a list of all the things you like to do that make you feel happy. For example:

• Take a walk in nature.

• Play with your children or pets.

- Read an uplifting book.

- Watch a comedy.

- Call a friend to get a cup of coffee.

- Write in a journal about all the things you are grateful for, including the gifts of insight.

- Take time to pray for divine guidance.

- Meditate, practice yoga, or simply treat yourself to any healthy, pleasurable activity that brings you joy.

If you have a challenge with feeling self-love and acceptance, you may have to practice it as you would any new skill or habit. When you behave as if you are in a loving supportive relationship with yourself, you will experience self-love, whether or not the relationship with your partner ends.

As you take steps to resolve inner conflict, analyze your needs and desires, empower yourself with life-affirming visualizations, and practice self-acceptance. Do things for yourself with an attitude of gratitude for yourself and all those who you encounter. Your internal emotional state will improve. The insights you receive about the part you play in your love partnership will inspire you to consciously make changes to enhance your relationships. When you demonstrate to your loved one that you are resolving your inner conflicts and achieving inner peace, the dynamics of relating will change. Surprisingly, you may inspire your partner to open his or her heart to more love.

To provide further support in this inner journey, consider meeting with a trained therapist who can help you achieve insight and emotional healing. Once you have worked on yourself and healed from the inside out, you can welcome a healthy, loving, committed relationship. The tools in this book can help you turn conflict into intimacy and a genuine love connection.

In summary, healing from the inside out is a process that takes you through the following steps:

- Observe your internal conflict.

- Accept yourself and the situation.

- Practice forgiveness of yourself and your partner.

- Love yourself.

- Clarify what you desire in your love life.

- Imagine harmony and love in your relationship.

- Act in a way that satisfies your relationship desires.

FIGHTING FOR LOVE EXERCISES:

1. Describe an internal conflict that you have in a past or present relationship.

2. How can you show compassion for yourself and accept the situation as it is?

3. What do you need to forgive yourself and your partner?

4. What do you desire in your love life now?

5. If you visualized love and harmony in your relationship, what would it look like?

6. What can you do to bring more love into your relationship?

Whenever you see darkness, there is extraordinary opportunity for the light to burn brighter.

– Bono

"I have a GPS device for each of you. The next time you drift apart,
these will help you find your way back to each other."

HARMONY

Harmony is pure love, for love is a concerto.

— Lope De Vega

M arci Shimoff in her book, *Love for No Reason*, wrote, "When you write a book on any topic, all of your issues about that subject will come up to be healed." We can attest to that! Writing and editing our chapters individually and as a team, forced us to delve into our own feelings, experiences, and memories about love. We had to walk our talk and, at times, address conflicting ideas and perspectives. We had to take time from our writing to process and create a joint vision for the project. Clearly, we both wanted to bring more love to the planet. In the process, we discovered what it meant to fight for love. We spent hours analyzing our former and present partners and questioned each other's beliefs about relationships.

It has been said that we teach best what we most need to learn. We are constantly reminded to fight for love and fight against anything that would keep us from getting the love we deserve. That involved actively changing ourselves and transforming our love relationships.

Leonard: After being single and divorced for nineteen years, my connection with Ingrid opened my heart to love again. Ironically, after three years of an intimate relationship, we are reviewing our goals and needs and respectfully working this out, while continuing to love and appreciate each other. I have come to realize that all situations and relationships can end in love, no matter what. Every relationship offers gifts, if I am determined to see them. One of the major gifts I continually receive is the realization that all relationships, be they personal or professional, need love. Some relationships last a lifetime; others have a limited life span. Yet all relationships ask us to fight for love. As Mari and I have said countless times, love is the only thing worth fighting for.

Mari: My relationship with my husband, Lloyd, has reaped the benefits of the writing of this book. We practiced the techniques and tools to help us connect and transform our conflicts, sometimes with grace and, at other times, not so much. But I noticed that as I expanded my attitude of gratitude, I noticed that he also became more appreciative. When I showed more tenderness, so did he. After twenty-seven years together, which include fifteen years of marriage, we recently renewed our vows in a spiritual ceremony with twenty other couples. Unbeknownst to me, Lloyd had frozen the Hawaiian tealeaf leis that we wore at our wedding and hidden them in the back of the freezer behind some aging frozen fish he had caught. The morning of our recommitment, he defrosted the leis and surprised me with them at the ceremony. Thank God they didn't pick up the fish smell! We lovingly draped them on each other, looked into each other's teary eyes, and softly renewed our vows, which we sealed with a kiss. I felt like a bride again as we recommitted to nourish and cherish one another. I am grateful for what I have learned in writing this book and how it has made me more conscious to fight against anything that gets in the way of love.

Leonard and Mari: In our relationship as coauthors and friends, we began to collaborate with the original intention of quickly writing a sixty-page eBook on conflict resolution for couples. We thought we could do it in a couple of months. As it turned out, the project had its own timetable. This book became our teacher. It forced us to learn about and respect each other's boundaries, acknowledge our differences, clarify our individual needs and preferences, and create harmony that incorporated our unique perspectives. It wasn't always easy because we had many differences, including upbringing, career backgrounds, writing styles, and gender, not to mention that we are both tenacious and assertive. Thankfully, we held similar spiritual beliefs, which served as our guiding force. Over time, we gained a deeper understanding about fighting for love. We even adopted some of each other's professional approaches when working with couples. We became the change that we wanted to see in the world as we harmonized our styles and our vision for bringing genuine love to relationships.

Just as musicians harmonize together to create pleasurable sounds, so can we harmonize our relationships to be pleasing, satisfying, and congenial. Love is harmony — a blending of two souls and hearts in rhythm. As we respectfully welcome our partner's different perspectives and lovingly listen to his or her melody of ideas, we join together as unique individuals to achieve an intimate melody.

Each musician must play his or her part to create a pleasing tune. Lovers must also harmonize to be in tune with love's song. From that place, we foster harmony in ourselves and merge with our loved one to create a symphony of intimacy. Harmony creates balance and accord when we shower our partner with acceptance, respect, dignity, gratitude, affection, devotion, and adoration.

In this book, we offer step-by-step approaches to enhance your love life — often using acronyms to make the strategies easier to remember. We leave you with one last acronym — **HARMONY**.

H — Hear your higher self and follow your inner GPS.

A — Ask for guidance from your intuition or through prayer and meditation.

R — Reflect on your past and analyze how it impacts the present.

M — Mindfully forgive and let go of past hurts.

O — Observe how good it feels to release judgments and criticism.

N — Nurture positive thoughts, feelings, and actions.

Y — Yearn for peace and serenity and visualize harmony.

Thank you for joining us on the journey to fight against anything that keeps you from getting the love you desire and deserve. Don't let anything divert you from the path of love. Turn conflict into intimacy.

Clothe yourselves with love, which binds everything together in perfect harmony.

Colossians 3:14.

TIPS AND IDEAS TO IGNITE YOUR PASSION

- Make it a priority to appreciate and be kind to yourself.

- Smile, listen deeply, and look lovingly in your sweetheart's eyes when communicating.

- Stop yourself before you judge, criticize, or blame.

- Take responsibility for your thoughts, emotions, and actions and keep them positive!

- Make time for romance and lovemaking.

- Show that you care by giving your partner what she/he needs to feel loved.

- Demonstrate his/her language of love with compliments, affection, quality time, acts of service, or gifts.

- Exercise or do sports together and take good care of your body, mind, and spirit.

- Evolve as a couple by reading aloud entertaining or inspiring books.

- Take a class, workshop, or seminar together.

- Hold hands at the movies, while walking in the park (or beach or lake), or cuddle while watching TV.

- Express an attitude of gratitude for what your partner does for you.

- Before you go to sleep, share with your partner three things for which you are grateful.

- Each morning and evening say, "I love you."

- At least once a day, or more, text or phone a message of love to each other.

- Plan date nights and new activities to add spice to your life.

- Share a spiritual practice that you both enjoy; pray together, stay together.

- Help each other with cooking and household responsibilities.

- Create time to play, engage with friends, and laugh.

- Plan vacations, even if they are short half-day adventures.

- Ask for what you want, not what you don't want.

- At least once or twice a year, share your dreams and desires for enhancing your love relationship and your life.

- When conflict does arise, pause, then speak low and slow while you practice the steps in solutioneering.

- Remember to give each other the AAA— attention, appreciation, and affection.

- Lighten up, laugh, and have fun!

BIBLIOGRAPHY

1. Amen, Daniel G., M.D., *The Brain in Love: 12 Lessons to Enhance Your Love Life*, New York: Three Rivers Press, 2007.

2. Banks, Amy, M.D., and Hirschman, Leigh Ann, *Wired to Connect: The Surprising Link Between Brain Science and Strong, Healthy Relationships*, New York: Jeremy P. Tarcher/Penguin, 2015.

3. Berger, Marcia Naomi, *Marriage Meetings for lasting love: 30 Minutes a Week to the Relationship You've Always Wanted*, California: New World Library, 2014.

4. Brown, Dr. Margot E., Kickstart *Your Relationship Now! Move On or Move Out*, USA: Brown & Brown, 2014.

5. Campolo, Tony, *Choose Love not Power: How to Right the World's Wrongs from a Place of Weakness*, California: Regal, 2009.

6. Cates, Regina, *Lead with Your Heart: Creating a Life of Love, Compassion, and Purpose*, Texas: Hierophant Publishing, 2014.

7. Chapman, Gary, *The 5 Love Languages: The Secret to Love that Lasts*, Chicago: Northfield Publishing, 2010.

8. Christensen, Andrew, PhD.; Doss, Brian D., PhD.; Jacobson, Neil S., PhD., *Reconcilable Differences, Second Edition: Rebuild Your Relationship by Rediscovering the Partner You Love – without Losing Yourself*: New York: Gilford Press, 2014.

9. Cloke, Kenneth, *The Dance of Opposites: Explorations in Mediation, Dialogue and Conflict Resolution Systems Design*, Texas: GoodMedia Press, 2013.

10. Creager, Todd, *Love, Sex & Karaoke: 52 Ways to Ignite Your Love Life*, USA: Todd Creager, 2015.

11. Crum, Thomas, *The Magic of Conflict: Turning a Life of Work into a Work of Art*, New York: Simon and Schuster, 1987.

12. Eddy, Bill, *BIFF: Quick Responses to High Conflict People, Their Personal Attacks, Hostile Email and Social Media Meltdowns*, USA: High Conflict Institute Press, 2011.

13. Eddy, Bill, *It's All Your Fault! 12 Tips for Managing People Who Blame Others for Everything*, USA: High Conflict Institute Press, 2009.

14. Eden, Donna, and Feinstein, David, *The Energies of Love: Invisible Keys to a Fulfilling Partnership: Transcending the Limits of Your Relationship,* New York: TarcherPerigee/Penguin Random House, 2014.

15. Francis, David Price, *Partners in Passion: Positively transform your intimate relationships by understanding the mystery of energy exchange,* USA: Kora Press, 2010.

16. Gattuso, Joan, *The Power of Forgiveness: Forgiving as a Path to Freedom,* New York: TarcherPerigee/ Penguin, 2014.

17. Gray, John, *Men are from Mars, Women are from Venus,* New York: Harper Collins, 1992.

18. Gottman, John M., Ph.D., *The Relationship Cure: A 5 Step Guide to Strengthening Your Marriage, Family, and Friendships,* New York: Three Rivers Press, 2001.

19. Hare, Jenny, *Secrets of Happy Relationships,* USA: McGraw-Hill, 2015.

20. Hendricks, Kathlyn, Ph.D.; Hendricks, Gay, Ph.D., *Lasting Love: The 5 Secrets of Growing a Vital, Conscious Relationship,* New York: Rodale Books, 2004.

21. Hendrix, Harville, *Getting the Love You Want: A Guide for Couples*, New York: St. Martin's Press, 2008.

22. Jeffers, Susan, Ph.D., *The Feel the Fear Guide to Lasting Love*, USA: Jeffers Press, 2005.

23. Johnson, Dr. Sue, *Hold Me Tight: Seven Conversations for Lifetime of Love*, New York: Little, Brown and Company, 2008.

24. Johnson, Dr. Sue, *Love Sense: The Revolutionary New Science of Romantic Relationships*, New York: Little, Brown and Company, 2013.

25. McGraw, Phillip C., Ph.D., *Relationship Rescue: A Seven-Step Strategy for Reconnecting with Your Partner*, New York: Hyperion, 2000.

26. Napthali, Sarah, *Buddhism for Couples: A Calm Approach to Relationships*, New York: Jeremy P. Tarcher/Penguin Random House, 2015.

27. Paul, Dr. Jordan & Dr. Margaret, *From Conflict to Caring: An In-depth Program for Creating Loving Relationships*, Minneapolis: Compcare Publications, 1989.

28. Psaris, Jett, and Lyons, Marlena S., *Undefended Love*, California: New Harbinger Publications, 2000.

29. Reble, Debra L., Ph.D., *Soul-Hearted Partnership: Creating the Ultimate Experience of Love, Passion, and Intimacy*, Ohio: HeartPaths Media, 2009

30. Siegel, Daniel, *Mindsight: The New Science of Personal Transformation*, New York: Bantam, 2011.

31. Schnarch, David, PhD, *Passionate Marriage: Love, Sex, and Intimacy in Emotionally Committed Relationships*, New York: W. W. Norton, 2009.

32. Solomon, Dr. Marion, *Lean on Me: The Power of Positive Dependency in Intimate Relationships*, New York: Simon & Schuster, 1994.

33. Tatkin, Stan, *Wired for Love: How Understanding Your Partner's Brain and Attachments Style Can Help You Defuse Conflict and Build a Secure Relationship*, California: New Harbinger Publications, 2012.

34. Ting-Toomey, Stella, and Chung, Leeva, *Understanding Intercultural Communication*, New York: Oxford University Press, 2011.

35. Tipping, Colin C., *Radical Forgiveness: Making Room for the Miracle*, Marietta, GA: Global 13 Publishers, 2002.

36. Turndorf, Jamie, *Kiss Your Fights Good-Bye: Dr. Love's 10 Simple Steps to Cooling Conflict and Rekindling Your Relationship*, USA: Hay House, 2014.

37. Ury, William, *Getting to Yes with Yourself and Other Worthy Opponents*, New York: HarperOne, 2015.

38. Wasser, Laura A., *It Doesn't Have to be That Way: How to Divorce Without Destroying Your Family or Bankrupting Yourself*, New York: St. Martin's Press, 2013.

39. Wish, Leslie Beth, *Smart Relationships: How Successful Women Can Find True Love*, New Jersey: New Horizon Press, 2013.

ACKNOWLEDGEMENTS

Mari: I am grateful to Leonard for his humor, patience, insight, expertise, and for his authenticity and friendship. I am so thankful that he walks his talk and actively listened when my views were different from his.

I offer my love and gratitude to my husband Lloyd Boshaw for his patience, devotion, and support. He willingly practices the Fighting for Love tools so we can reconcile our differences.

Another dear collaborator, to whom I am grateful, is my wonderful supportive assistant and paralegal, Ann Huynh, who helps me attend to my clients, keep me on schedule, prepare and organize me for meetings, and keep me sane with her wit and wisdom.

Leonard: I am grateful for the opportunity to work with Mari. Her passion for healing conflict ignited my desire to collaborate and produce this book with her. Together, we fought for the best way to present this material, and in the process, deepened our friendship.

Creating a book also involves a community. There have been countless people who have supplied help, offered suggestions, and provided loving support. Clearly, the countless clients who Mari has mediated and Leonard has counseled provided life experiences that helped shape the material in the book.

We want to recognize and offer our heartfelt thanks to the following:

Our friend and colleague Bill Eddy, an attorney/mediator and therapist, who deeply understands and shares our commitment to heal couples in conflict.

Randy Glasbergen, whose cartoons gave levity and laughter to our work. He's now making the angels laugh in heaven.

Bryan Frank, who gave us the creative title for the book.

Our graphic artist, Fiona Jayde, who grasped the essence of our book and clothed our words in a powerful package.

Mary Harris, our editor, for her eagle eyes, her wordsmithing, and her wonderful support.

Our interior designer, Tamara Cribley, who helped create a polished and professional book.

And to all those who supported us along the way: Inspirit Center for Spiritual Living, Leonard's men's group, Ingrid Starrs, Daniel Midson-Short, Kevin Daniels, Toni Hull, Anne Larson, Eva Quan, Felice Williams, and Karin Crilly.

And finally, to our loving families and friends, who cheered us on.

ABOUT RANDY GLASBERGEN, CARTOONIST

We are grateful to Randy Glasbergen for his wonderful cartoons that added a little levity to our book. Randy was one of America's most widely and frequently published cartoonists and humorous illustrators. Businesses, schools, and organizations of all sizes use Glasbergen Cartoons to help them deliver their message with humor and a smile. Randy's cartoons are seen all over the world in newspapers, magazines, greeting cards, books, calendars, advertising textbooks, social media, and more.

Randy began his professional cartoonist career at age 15 and began freelancing full-time after a year of journalism studies in Utica, New York. Aside from a year spent as a staff humor writer at Hallmark Cards in Kansas City, he had been a full-time freelance cartoonist since 1976. Sadly, Randy passed away on August 11, 2015, but his comedic view of life continues to live on through his cartoons.

www.glasbergen.com

ABOUT MARI FRANK

Mari Frank, Esq. CIPP, is an attorney/ mediator, author, professional speaker and radio host. She is the author of *Negotiation Breakthroughs,* co-author of *Stepping Stones to Success,* and several other books. She has written dozens of published articles about negotiations and conflict transformation. Mari trains lawyers for the State Bar of California and has taught conflict resolution at the University of California, Irvine, Brandman University, and Western State College of Law.

She is the radio host of *Fighting for Love* on KUCI, 88.9 FM in Irvine, California. She hosted her own PBS TV special, and she's been interviewed on numerous national TV and radio shows. She's been featured in *The Daily Journal,* the *Los Angeles Times,* the *Orange County Register,* and the *ABA Journal* (the American Bar Association publication), and quoted in dozens of national newspapers. Mari mediates in her private practice in Laguna Niguel, CA and for the Orange County Superior Court.

Mari@MariFrank.com

www.MariFrank.com

www.conflicthealing.com

ABOUT LEONARD SZYMCZAK

Leonard Szymczak, MSW, LCSW is a writer, international speaker, psychotherapist, and life coach. For the past 40 years, he has worked in both Australia and America counseling individuals, couples, and families to resolve conflict. He was Director of the Family Therapy Program at the Marriage and Family Centre in Sydney, Australia, where he managed the counseling services and trained family therapists. He later served as a senior affiliate therapist with the Family Institute at Northwestern University.

He is the author of *The Roadmap Home: Your GPS to Inner Peace*, an Amazon Bestseller, as well as the novels, *Cuckoo Forevermore* and *Kookaburra's Last Laugh*, lighthearted satires on psychotherapy. He ghostwrote and produced the memoir *Silence and Secrets* for a Holocaust survivor. He is an international speaker and workshop presenter and maintains a counseling and coaching practice in Orange County, CA. Leonard is the proud father of two adult children.

leonard@leonardsz.com

www.leonardsz.com

www.facebook.com/leonardszymczakauthor

FOR MORE INFORMATION ON
FIGHTING FOR LOVE

www.Fightingforlovenow.com

info@Fightingforlovenow.com

fightingforlovenow@gmail.com

www.facebook.com/FightingForLoveNow

Made in the USA
San Bernardino, CA
26 May 2020